Advance Praise for Wing Chun In-Depth . . .

Aristotle once said, "the most difficult thing in the world is to discover and know yourself." One way to do this is to interact with a real friend who will play the role of a mirror and help you "see" yourself and assist you in achieving self-realization, self-confidence, and self-control.

Reading Plato's dialogues, we often cannot recognize who is the true author (Aristotle the master, or Plato the student). This matters less that the content itself. Something similar is happening in this book. What really matters is that Wing Chun is preserved and transferred to future generations. Like Plato, these authors invite you to question and analyze yourself by accepting current circumstances and remaining focused to find your own truth and to deal with the complexity and challenges of your own life. This book will help you discover your inner self, allowing your skills and abilities to be revealed and your imagination explored.

Wing Chun In-Depth begins with the origins and history of the Wing Chun system. It explores the contributions of Ip Man and Bruce Lee through the social and political environments of their times. The authors focus not only on sophisticated martial skills but on principles, mental values, attitudes, and philosophies that these masters taught for success in life. It continues with an examination of Wing Chun skills including the economy of motion, effort, and natural reactions with forward energy. The work is also precisely illustrated with hundreds of enhanced photographs.

The authors complete this book by offering the readers various strategies on how Wing Chun's universal principles can work as a stabilizing force in life. Wing Chun is a way of thinking. It helps overcome anger, stress, bias, and mental blocks. It replaces them with calmness, charm, and intelligence so that we can confront the most difficult opponent: ourselves. In Wing Chun, every obstacle is an opportunity to find a natural way. This book will inspire the remarkable journey of Wing Chun and bring out the very best in all who take it.

—**Vasileios Manousakis** Colonel GR (A)

If you are looking for a book on Wing Chun that covers both the practical aspects of applying the techniques in combat as well as the philosophical side of the martial art, then this is the book for you. I have read many books on Wing Chun, and this is by far one of the most comprehensive and well-written books I have come across.

Loukas Kastrounis has been teaching martial arts for over thirty years to many martial artists of different styles, law enforcement officers, security firms, and the military at home and overseas. He is a highly creative instructor with a unique approach to training that helps students achieve their goals quickly and effectively.

Wing Chun In-Depth: Skills for Combat, Strategies for Life is a must-read for anyone passionate about Wing Chun and martial arts. This is one of those books you will be able to reference time and time again. I highly recommend this book for everyone!

—**Lafayette Harris**, Wing Chun martial arts instructor

A solidly researched, beautifully narrated deep dive into the philosophical, historical, and technical aspects of Wing Chun. Fascinating history combined with great narration and revealing insights that make Wing Chun relevant for all of life's challenges. Highly recommended if you love history, martial arts, and strategy.

—**Erwan Le Corre**, author of *The Practice of Natural Movement*

I was fascinated to understand how Wing Chun practitioners can gain mechanical advantages through natural movement and gain *freedom* through imitation and repetition. It's as though the practitioner is a work of art [becoming] a masterpiece. Reading the history of Wing Chun practitioners drew me in deeply, a veritable who's-who of Wing Chun.

—**Eric Brown**, former US Navy SEAL,
Naval Special Warfare Center Instructor of the Year (1993)

Wing Chun In-Depth

Wing Chun In-Depth

Skills for Combat, Strategies for Life

MUNAWAR ALI KARIM

LOUKAS KASTROUNIS

YMAA Publication Center
Wolfeboro, NH USA

YMAA Publication Center, Inc.
PO Box 480
Wolfeboro, NH 03894
800-669-8892 • www.ymaa.com • info@ymaa.com

ISBN 9781594399275 (print)
ISBN 9781594399282 (e-book)
ISBN 9781594399299 (hardcover)

Copyright © 2023 by Munawar Ali Karim and Loukas Kastrounis
All rights reserved including the right of reproduction in whole or in part in any form.

Cover design by Axie Breen
Photos provided by the authors unless otherwise indicated.
Illustrations copyright © 2023 by Munawar Ali Karim
Edited by Doran Hunter
This book typeset in Adobe Garamond and Myriad

20230309

Publisher's Cataloging in Publication

Title: Wing chun in-depth : skills for combat, strategies for life / Munawar Ali Karim, Loukas Kastrounis.

Description: Wolfeboro, NH : YMAA Publication Center, Inc., [2023] | Includes bibliographical references.

Identifiers: ISBN: 9781594399275 (softcover) | 9781594399299 (hardcover) | 9781594399282 (ebook) | LCCN: 2022951533

Subjects: LCSH: Kung fu. | Kung fu--History. | Kung fu--Training. | Martial arts--History. | Martial arts--Training. | Hand-to-hand fighting, Oriental--History. | Martial artists--Biography. | Qi (Chinese philosophy) | Martial arts--Psychological aspects. | Self-actualization (Psychology) | Self-realization. | Self-control. | BISAC: SPORTS & RECREATION / Martial Arts / General. | SPORTS & RECREATION / History.

Classification: LCC: GV1114.7 .K37 2023 | DDC: 796.815/9--dc23

The authors and publisher of the material are NOT RESPONSIBLE in any manner whatsoever for any injury which may occur through reading or following the instructions in this manual.

The activities physical or otherwise, described in this manual may be too strenuous or dangerous for some people, and the reader(s) should consult a physician before engaging in them.

Warning: While self-defense is legal, fighting is illegal. If you don't know the difference you'll go to jail because you aren't defending yourself. You are fighting—or worse. Readers are encouraged to be aware of all appropriate local and national laws relating to self-defense, reasonable force, and the use of weaponry, and act in accordance with all applicable laws at all times. Understand that while legal definitions and interpretations are generally uniform, there are small—but very important—differences from state to state and even city to city. To stay out of jail, you need to know these differences. Neither the authors nor the publisher assumes any responsibility for the use or misuse of information contained in this book.

Nothing in this document constitutes a legal opinion nor should any of its contents be treated as such. While the authors believe that everything herein is accurate, any questions regarding specific self-defense situations, legal liability, and/or interpretation of federal, state, or local laws should always be addressed by an attorney at law.

When it comes to martial arts, self-defense, and related topics, no text, no matter how well written, can substitute for professional, hands-on instruction. **These materials should be used for academic study only.**

Printed in USA.

Contents

Dedication and Acknowledgements — vii
Preface — ix
Introduction — xi

Part One: The Lineage — 1

1: Through The Tempests of History
   China at the Time of Grandmaster Ip Man's Birth (1900s) — 3

2: Alive and Well
   Bringing Wing Chun out of Myth and Into History — 9

3: Growing and Continuing
   Two Legendary Students of Grandmaster Ip Man — 19

4: In the Present and on to the Future
   From Sifu Wong Shun Leung to Sifu Loukas Kastrounis — 29

Part Two: The System — 37

5: What's the Big Idea?
   A Concise Overview of Wing Chun — 39

6: Siu Nim Tau
   The First Form, the Last Form — 43

7: Chi-Sau
   The Heart and Soul of Wing Chun — 97

Part Three: Up Close — 105

8: Master Class 1
   Training to Fight Without Fighting — 107

9: Master Class 2
   Avoiding the Mexican Stand-Off — 121

10: Master Class 3
   "No Technique As Technique" — 141

Part Four: Strategies for Life — 177

11: Beyond Fighting
   What Wing Chun Can Teach Us About Life — 179

Afterword: Closing Thoughts on Wing Chun — 195
About the Authors — 197

Dedication and Acknowledgements

Dedicated to all martial artists of all styles and systems. We hope this book will help you to understand better what you are practicing.

From Sifu Loukas Kastrounis

Special thanks to Munawar for bringing my teaching into a book, to my teacher Nino Bernardo for his guidance. Many thanks to Nick Radcliffe (my first-generation student who started training with me in 1995 and is still with me to this day) for participating in the illustrations and demonstrations in this book. Thanks to my students, old and new, for inspiring me to transmit my Wing Chun to future generations. Thanks to my Kung-fu brothers for the many years we trained together at The Basement in London. Kung-fu is my passion and while I have spent many hours and years of my life training I know that my family have been patient enough to allow me to continue my life's work. I want to especially thank my children—Maria, George, Paula, Leonidas, and my wife Jenny for bearing with me patiently throughout all of this time.

From Munawar Ali Karim

For the men and women of Wing Chun, past, present, and future
for my students at Deenway Dojo
for those who seek the Way
and for R., S., and H.

With special thanks to Sifu Loukas for entrusting me to set down in writing his life's work and for teaching me his Wing Chun; and to Mobashar for all the roads we have travelled together in search of truth in the martial arts. Thanks also to Fotis for listening to an early draft of this work during a short training excursion to Greece. The long hours spent researching and writing this book would not have been possible without the patience, care, and affection of my wife Asia and the unconditional love and self-sacrifice of my parents. To them I remain eternally grateful and can never repay their favor.

Preface

Dear Reader,

This book is the product of an interaction between a Wing Chun master and one of his students. When Sifu Loukas Kastrounis asked me to write down his teaching in the form of a book I felt both honored and humbled. Honored, because it was a sign of the great deal of trust that my teacher was placing in me. Humbled, because I recognized the enormity of what was being asked. Over the four or five years that followed I tried to pay close attention to Loukas's words, teaching methods, and interactions with his students and his peers. I also sought as much as possible to craft a work that translated the spirit, beauty, and "rawness" of his Wing Chun teaching to the literary medium. This, I felt, was the most honest way to give expression to the richness of what Loukas has to offer as a Wing Chun teacher.

The "rawness" of his teaching lies in its uncut honesty. Observing Sifu Loukas delivering a seminar or teaching a class, it becomes clear that he is openly sharing his Wing Chun as he received it himself. Such teachers are rare in this age, and for this reason I felt it was important to trace Loukas's lineage and share the story of Wing Chun as far as it is known. This is done in the first part of the book. The intention here is to inspire you to commence, or to continue, your journey into this beautiful and profound practice that is rooted in Chinese heritage and tradition. The second part of the book provides a summary of Wing Chun as a system. This section is deliberately concise, like Wing Chun itself. It is designed to provide an overview of Wing Chun as a whole, serving as a ready reference for beginners and a useful reminder for more experienced practitioners. The third part of the book looks closely at how Wing Chun practice and principles translate into real fighting skills. The final and concluding part of the book explores the strategic fruits of Wing Chun as a practice which provides not only skills for combat, but also strategies for life. Within it are gleanings of wisdom and hidden treasures for everyday life inside and outside the kwoon, the office, the school, the dojo, and the home. The narrative voice in this book fluctuates between Loukas and myself. Sometimes the teacher speaks for himself directly. And other times he speaks through the interpretive voice of his student.

If you enjoy this book and benefit from what it has to offer; if it inspires you to take up Wing Chun, or continue your practice from a new perspective; or if it sheds light on how Wing Chun provides strategies for life, not just for combat; then this effort has not been in vain, and I can rest assured that the book has achieved its purpose.

Munawar Karim
Reading, Berkshire

INTRODUCTION

The competent Wing Chun practitioner moves with a sophisticated understanding of body mechanics. He responds to dangerous forces with mechanical efficiency. He appears to effortlessly redirect hostile force to a position of personal advantage. He understands how to align his body and limbs correctly to produce maximum leverage and remove an incoming threat to his centerline. The scientific term for this is mechanical advantage. But don't be fooled: while the Wing Chun practitioner does indeed have a deep, intuitive grasp of body mechanics, his body is not in fact responding mechanically. It is responding naturally and freely. The Wing Chun adept is not a slave to his art—although his path to "mastery" began with imitation. His art is now his. He owns it and it's his guide in difficult situations.

There is little margin of error in following that guide. But surprisingly this is not an art that teaches techniques. Wing Chun is a martial art that focuses on principles, energy work, body mechanics, and efficiency of movement. There are only three hand forms in Wing Chun: *Siu Nim Tau*, *Chum Kiu*, and *Biu Jee*. With the diligent practice of these forms and patient self-reflection, a Wing Chun student is guided on a life-long journey of self-discovery that teaches much more than how to deal with physical threats. At its essence Wing Chun teaches us how to find our balance when most people have already lost their own. It teaches us how to respond to stupid questions with intelligent answers. It teaches us when to walk away and when to walk on. It teaches us how to carry on moving forward when everything is dark around us. And for these reasons it is much more than a science. It is a tradition whose roots lie forgotten in the history of ancient China, but whose branches extend throughout the world. There are many blossoms on this tree but few fruits. In the life-long work of Sifu Loukas Kastrounis the tradition evolves, and the fruits are plenty…

PART ONE
THE LINEAGE

*"Many words, few deeds—that is the fault of man.
Many blossoms, few fruits—that is the work of Heaven…"*

—*Traditional aphorism*

Part One traces the lineage of Sifu Loukas Kastrounis's Wing Chun schools from the mythical origins of the art before the 1700s, through the turbulent history of the birth of the Chinese state in the nineteenth and twentieth centuries, and into the modern world.

It recounts the life of some of the great teachers in this unbroken chain and places their work in the context of the trying circumstances in which they lived.

It is presented to the reader as a means of sharing with them the beauty and pedigree of the Wing Chun system. And it is offered as a token of gratitude to those Wing Chun teachers—past, present, and future— who have given so much of themselves to enrich this practice and share it with others with sincerity and passion.

1

THROUGH THE TEMPESTS OF HISTORY
China at the Time of Grandmaster Ip Man's Birth (1900s)

Louis Lassen is serving up the world's first hamburgers in New Haven, Connecticut, and the Wright Brothers are setting the stage for the first controlled power flight. J. M. Barrie is working on a play entitled *Peter Pan* and the British Labour Party has just been founded. In a few years' time Albert Einstein will publish his theory of relativity and Henry Ford will produce the first Model T. Shortly after that the unsinkable *Titanic* will sink; a Duke in Europe will be assassinated, igniting the First World War; and the Arabs will revolt against the Ottoman Empire. It is the early 1900s. The Old World is receding into the past and the modern world is slowly emerging. The Age of Empires is unraveling. The Ottoman Empire in the West and the Qing Empire in the East will soon crumble under the weight of these changes. But along with them, the much younger Western-colonial empires will also come to a swift end: Britain is struggling to hold on to its global imperial possessions and is engaged in a bloody war with the Boers in Africa. In India there is great resentment against the British Raj. The French in Tunisia, the British in Egypt, and the Italians in Ethiopia (and then later in Libya) are finding that the locals would much rather be independent of their colonial masters. Meanwhile Britain, France, Germany, the United States, Russia, and Japan are all engaged in a "Great Game" to take, by hook or by crook, as much of the riches and resources from the decaying Qing Empire of China as they can.

In the West great leaps are being made in technology and science. Marconi is about to transmit the first wireless signal acrojss the Atlantic; Pierre and Marie Curie have already discovered radium; Wilhelm Rontgen has identified X-rays; Alexander Bell has invented the telephone. The great science and learning of the East, and particularly of China, that once produced such world-changing inventions like the printing press, gunpowder, silk, and paper, and from whence the Great Admiral Zheng-He's fleet once circumnavigated the entire globe at a time when most Europeans still believed the world was flat—that East and that great Chinese civilization seem irrelevant in this brave new world of European dominance. To most Europeans, and to the Japanese, Americans, and Russians, China seems very much like a culture with very little to offer the world—except for its hoard of treasures and ancient artifacts, which are ripe for plunder.

The old Chinese ways are no match for the overpowering might and firepower of the foreign invaders. The old Qing Dynasty that has been ruling China since 1644 seems powerless to stop the pillage and plundering of the foreigners.

Ironically, the Qing Dynasty also began its life as a foreign power. Following the collapse of the Ming, Manchu chieftains from the plains and forests northeast of China took over the kingdom. That was more than three hundred years ago. The Manchus were considered "non-Chinese" because they did not belong to any of the many ethnicities that traditionally made up Chinese society. Commoners and elites took up arms against them. Many great Kung-fu legends, movies, and folktales have their origins in this time; Wing Chun is no exception. It was the Qing who destroyed the fabled Shaolin Temple for fear that it was harboring anti-Qing rebels. Later generations of Chinese learned to adapt to the Qing dynasty, and the Manchus themselves adopted many Chinese ways.

By the early 1800s traditional Chinese civilization was at a high point under the Manchu rulers. But as the 1800s drew to an end, and as the power and might of foreign nations grew due to advancements in technology, science, trade and warfare, China began to be derided and mocked by the colonial powers.

From 1840 the British engaged in a war to protect opium imports into China, and by 1842 many Chinese were afflicted with addiction to the drug:

> *[Chinese] officials confiscated some 20,000 chests of opium held in British warehouses in Guanzou (Canton) smuggled there by British merchants as payment from India for exports of tea, porcelain, and silk. Looking for a way to end Chinese trade restrictions [on illegal drug trafficking], Britain responded in 1840 by sending sixteen gunboats to besiege Chinese coastal cities. In 1842, the Chinese were forced to sign the treaty of Nanjing, followed by the British Supplementary Treaty of the Bogue in 1843. Hong Kong was ceded to Britain and the treaty ports of Guangzhou, Jinmen, Fuzhou, Ningbo, and Shanghai were opened up to British trade and residence.*[1]

But the humiliation of the Chinese was just beginning. In 1856, Britain renewed hostilities with China following a search by Chinese officials of a British registered ship. By 1857 British and French troops had taken Guanzhou and Tianjin, and in 1858 China was forced to sign treaties with Britain, France, Russia, and the USA opening up more ports to foreign exploitation and guaranteeing foreign merchants and Christian missionaries freedom to travel into the Chinese interior with impunity. Even as Chinese opposition grew, the allied foreign armies marched right into Beijing and burned down the imperial Summer Palace. Britain and the other Western armies then forced the Chinese to legalize drug trafficking by signing the Peking Convention, which allowed them to import opium into China without interference from the Chinese authorities. In short, the Qing dynasty had proven powerless to protect its people from foreign interference.

---

1. *Encyclopedia of World History* (Oxford: Oxford University Press, 1998).

> *Western merchants sold manufactured goods that competed with Chinese industries; their missionaries competed with Chinese literati for moral and religious leadership in the countryside; and their armies and navies repeatedly proved themselves superior to China's, raising fundamental questions about what, if anything, China should copy from these aggressive foreigners.*[2]

This was the world that Ip Man was born into in the early 1890s. The Empress Dowager Cixi controlled the Qing throne on behalf of her young son. The Opium Wars had devastated large parts of the country. Western powers seemed to threaten Chinese culture and society. And the foreigners' lack of respect for Chinese culture and ways was a painful humiliation for many Chinese. The dowager empress had passionately loved the Summer Palace. She was a teenage concubine to the Emperor in 1860 when the British and French looted its treasures—hacking off jewels and pearls embedded in the intricate furniture, tearing off the silk screens and rich brocades, and making off with its precious artifacts. As dowager empress she tried to appease the foreign powers and gave in to their outrageous treaties—she knew painfully well what it meant to incur their wrath. But she could not forgive or forget the day the British deliberately set the Summer Palace aflame and burned it to ashes. Even the French had not dared go that far. And so while negotiating with the foreigners she also gave covert support to a secret society calling itself "The Harmonious Fists" (I-He Chu'an).

China has always had a rich tradition of secret societies and sects combining religious and spiritual beliefs, rigorous martial arts practice, and opposition to the ruling elite. Centuries before the Harmonious Fists and the Qing dynasty, there were secret sects such as the White Lotus and the Pa-Kua. The White Lotus sect supported the Red Turban Revolution in the 1300s against the Mongol-founded Yuan dynasty. Their support for an ex-Buddhist monk, Chu-Yuan Chang, helped him become the first Ming emperor. In 1394 he issued a decree against the White Lotus sect—the very group that had helped him into power—recognizing, as all Chinese rulers have, that a secret group of trained martial artists with strong political views present dangers to their authority.

The Pa-Kua based their spiritual and martial arts practices on the *I-Ching*—the famous book of Chinese divination. After a protracted rebellion in the 1780s north of the Yellow River, where the Pa-Kua society was based, a decree was issued for the sect to be crushed. It is not clear if the Pa-Kua society or the martial art by the same name (Bagua), came first. But undoubtedly the two have an intricately related history.

Bagua, however, was just one of many martial arts associated with secret societies and the overthrow of tyrants. The Qing dynasty succeeded in alienating many people with its rigid class-based system and practices deliberately designed to humiliate the indigenous Chinese ethnicities. Among these was to force Chinese men to shave part of their heads and wear

---

2. Patricia Buckley Ebrey, *The Cambridge Illustrated History of China* (Cambridge: Cambridge University Press, 2010), 220.

long braided ponytails. When people resisted this practice they were executed. This was a clear statement to the new subject populations: Manchu ways are superior. (Later, foreign powers would mock these hairstyles, and later still, Kung-fu movies would make them iconic.)

Among the many secret societies that emerged to resist and overthrow the Qing dynasty was a group of early Wing Chun practitioners whose exploits are not easily unraveled from cultural legends of martial arts heroes (see below). What is quite clear, however, is that they often shared a common slogan: "Overthrow the Qing, restore the Ming."

And so there is little doubt that these early martial-arts based secret societies that had for so long played a part in the overthrow (or attempted overthrow) of Chinese rulers influenced the formation of the I-He-Chu'an, The Harmonious Fists, in the late 1800s. There is also little doubt that the Dowager Empress Cixi—as representative of the now decaying Qing dynasty—needed to channel the discontent of the Harmonious Fists away from her and towards a common enemy. The Boxers, as they came to be known in the West, may have started off opposing the Qing dynasty just as the martial-arts-based secret societies of their predecessors had done in the past. But, encouraged no doubt by the dowager empress, they came to channel their discontent increasingly against the foreigners that were looting China of its glorious treasures while inundating the population with opium and (in their eyes at least) degrading Chinese culture by propagating Christianity. In other words, as the Qing dynasty decayed, new tyrants had stepped into the shoes of the Manchus—Britain, France, Germany, Japan, Russia, and the USA.

And so the Boxers began attacking missionaries, foreigners, and their families. The dowager empress was uncertain how to respond but finally began to support them in secret, encouraging them to march on the foreign legations in Beijing in the hope of weakening their control over China.

In 1898, conservative, anti-foreign forces won control of the Chinese government and persuaded the Boxers to drop their opposition to the Qing dynasty and unite with it in destroying the foreigners. The governor of the province of Shandong began to enroll Boxer bands as local militia groups, changing their name from Yihequan to Yihetuan ("Righteous and Harmonious Militia"), which sounded semiofficial. Many of the Qing officials at this time apparently began to believe that Boxer rituals actually did make them impervious to bullets, and, in spite of protests by the Western powers, they and Cixi, the ruling empress dowager, continued to encourage the group.

Christian missionary activities helped provoke the Boxers; Christian converts flouted traditional Chinese ceremonies and family relations; and missionaries pressured local officials to side with Christian converts—who were often from the lower classes of Chinese society—in local lawsuits and property disputes. By late 1899 the Boxers were openly attacking Chinese Christians and Western missionaries. By May 1900, Boxer bands were roaming the countryside around the capital at Beijing. Finally, in early June an international relief force of some 2,100 men was dispatched from the northern port of Tianjin to Beijing. On June 13 the empress dowager ordered imperial forces to block the advance of the foreign troops, and the small relief column was turned back. Meanwhile, in Beijing the Boxers burned churches and foreign residences and killed suspected Chinese Christians on sight. On June 17 the foreign powers seized the Dagu forts on the coast in order to restore access from Beijing to Tianjin. The next day the empress dowager ordered that all foreigners be killed. The German minister was murdered, and the other foreign ministers and their families and staff, together with hundreds of Chinese Christians, were besieged in their legation quarters and in the Roman Catholic cathedral in Beijing.

Imperial viceroys in the central Yangtze River (Chang Jiang) valley and in South China ignored government orders and suppressed anti-foreign outbreaks in their jurisdiction. They thus helped establish the myth that the war was not the policy of the Chinese government but was a result of a native uprising in the northeast, the area to which the disorders were mainly confined.

On August 14, 1900, an international force finally captured Beijing, relieving the foreigners and Christians besieged there since June 20. While foreign troops looted the capital, the empress dowager and her court fled westward to Xi'an in Shaanxi province, leaving behind a few imperial princes to conduct the negotiations. After extensive discussions, a protocol was finally signed in September 1901, ending the hostilities and providing for reparations to be made to the foreign powers.[3]

The Boxers, or anyone associated with them, were executed en masse and thousands of people—Chinese, foreigners, soldiers, and civilians—all lost their lives. The foreign powers used this as an opportunity to further exploit China and operate as they pleased on Chinese soil. The Boxers who survived disappeared into obscurity—though some may have fled to Taiwan . . .

Ip Man was around six years old at this time. China was in trauma. There was great tension between traditional Chinese culture and the modern, aggressively imposed ways of the foreigners. The Boxers had been crushed. Martial Arts, and those who practiced them, were regarded with great suspicion and mocked by the foreign nations that were now masters of the Chinese. Foreigners, for the most part, sneered at the Chinese and despised them. Little surprise then that in the early decades of the 1900s Chinese masters were reluctant to share their traditional martial arts with foreigners. For martial artists like Ip Man, the art that had

---

3. *Encyclopedia Britannica*, "Boxer Rebellion," http://www.britannica.com/EBchecked/topic/76364/Boxer-Rebellion 040814.

been handed down by their teachers was a priceless treasure of Chinese culture. All their young lives they had experienced life under foreigners that ridiculed the Chinese people, occupied their lands, and methodically stripped China of its riches. It is to the credit of some of Ip Man's students (most famously Bruce Lee and Wong Shong Leung) that they would go on to share this rich and precious part of their culture with the wider world. Moreover, it says a lot about Ip Man's character that although he did not teach foreigners himself, he did not prevent his students from doing so. And so it is important for those of us who are now heirs to this tradition to preserve it, nurture it, and pass it on to others faithfully, realizing just what a great gift we have been given and how privileged we are to be entrusted with this treasure.

2
ALIVE AND WELL
Bringing Wing Chun Out of Myth and into History

Ip Man was born in Foshan, Guangdong province—a once-thriving town at the heart of the Pearl River Delta, rich in iron deposits, manufacturing, and handicrafts. Foshan was also rich in martial arts practitioners. However, over time Foshan had grown less important and less wealthy as new port cities were opened up by the foreigners. The people of nearby Gunagzhou, who once upon a time were major consumers of Foshan exports, now had other sources to supply their needs. And yet in the early 1900s, with all that was happening elsewhere in China, Foshan was still a well-to-do city. The Boxer Rebellion had been crushed, foreign powers had a tighter grip on China than ever before, and martial-arts societies were considered with suspicion. Martial arts masters responded to these developments in different ways. Some continued the practice of their arts privately and no longer taught openly. Others practiced with small groups of close friends or family members. Still others attempted to distance martial arts from the subversive secret societies of the past. Perhaps most famous among these was the Jing Wu Athletic Association (founded around 1910), which sought to consolidate and preserve core elements of the Chinese martial arts and present them to modernity as a form of Chinese athletic pursuit on a par with boxing, fencing, and other "Western" sports.

But traditional martial arts are much more than physical exercises. Those who practice such arts are enriched by them, and if they become great practitioners of those arts, they go on to enrich them further still. Ip Man was destined to be one of these great masters.

*

It's 1910 in Foshan, Guangdong Province. A decade has passed since the Boxer Rebellion in the north. Some martial arts associations and schools are now teaching openly again. Among them is the Hung Sing Association specializing in Choy Li Fut Kung-fu and attracting many semi-skilled workers around Guangdong province. In the next ten years or so, the Jing Wu Association will also attract lots of followers with its modern presentation of the martial arts. The Jing Wu Association will leverage its connection with successful business owners to attract young, educated, middle-class students. There are smaller traditional schools of martial arts in Foshan too. Martial arts competitions and tests of strength are common. The pride of one's school, the skill of one's teacher, and the superiority of one's art are all at stake in such matches.

A small group of students start training at the Ip Man family's ancestral hall in Foshan's Main Street. Their teacher is an elderly man by the name of Chan Wah-Shun, also called "Money-Changer Wah" because of the currency-exchange business he used to operate in the past. Nowadays the old man teaches a style of Kung-fu called Wing Chun and practices herbal medicine. He learned both things from his teacher, Dr. Leung Jan, who used to operate an herbal clinic next door to Wah's money-changing shop. Apparently Dr. Leung had been a legendary fighter in his time, winning challenge matches but not taking many students. Perhaps this was because of the political climate of those times, with the Qing empire seeking out rebels and foreigners wary of "boxers," and his art was meant to be preserved secretly. Old Money-Changer Wah was not well educated. But he was Dr. Leung's neighbor and had earned his trust. And in his younger days he would repay that trust by further enhancing the respectability of Wing Chun in countless challenge matches and fights, earning himself and his art a fierce reputation.

But Chan Wah-Shun refuses to teach Ip Man. Ip Man's family owns the hall where Chan is teaching. Ip is obviously from a wealthy family. No doubt he has had a pampered upbringing. Martial Arts training requires effort and hard work. You have to be prepared to step out of your comfort zone if you want to learn. Wing Chun is not for everyone. Perhaps Chan Wah-Shun thinks the more sanitized Jing Wu Association is a better place for Ip Man where he can train with people from his own social class. But Ip Man is not easily put off. He wants to study traditional Kung-fu in the traditional way and he wants to study Wing Chun.

According to some accounts, Chan Wah-Shun attempts to get rid of Ip Man by demanding a large sum of money for tuition. Ip Man goes home, takes out his life savings, and comes back with the money. Chan Wah-Shun realizes that this young man is serious and agrees in the end to accept him as a student. Ip Man will be the last student Chan Wah-Shun accepts. He is already an old man now. Shortly before he passes away he puts one of his best students—Ng Jung So—in charge of Ip's training. We can imagine the scene: the old Wing Chun master has seen talent in his youngest disciple. Knowing he cannot teach him all he needs to know before he passes away, he turns to Ng Jung So, one of his best senior students. "Train him well," he says. "This boy has talent . . ."

*

The exploits of Dr. Leung Jan, Chah Wah-Shun's teacher, are the stuff movies are made of—quite literally. Countless popular stories, movies, and costume-dramas romanticize his life and martial arts skills. So far our story of the origins of Wing Chun has remained within the realms of known history. There are slight details people differ over: how old exactly was Ip Man when he began training with old Money-Changer Wah? Some say he was around seven years old, others say ten or thirteen. For how long did Wah-Shun train Ip Man before he died? Was it one or two years or more, or less? Despite these minor differences the story of Wing Chun's origins thus far remains firmly within known history. But the facts about Dr. Leung Jan's life are much less clear, largely because there are so many competing accounts.

What is known about him is that he took over his father's herbal clinic on Fai Jee Street in Foshan in the mid-1800s. This was, of course, about the same time that war was breaking out between China and Britain over the opium trade. An interesting oral account says that Leung Jan named his herbal clinic Hang Chai Tong ("Apricot Tea Hall") after the legends of folk-hero Wu Teng Feng, who was said to have treated thousands of poor people for free in the apricot forest where he lived.

In any case, it seems that Leung Jan learned Wing Chun from two members of a Red Boat Opera troupe—Leung Yee Tai and Wong Wah Bo. Leung Yee Tai, it is said, had learnt the six-and-a-half-point long pole technique from Abbott Chi Shin who had escaped from the Shaolin Temple when it was destroyed by an earlier Qing Emperor. For his part, Wong Wah Bo had studied Wing Chun from an herbalist by the name of Leung Lan Kwai. As enemies of the Qing, hiding out with the Red Boat Opera, both men came to know of each other's martial skills and collaborated to refine their techniques. And so they further improved Wing Chun and incorporated the six-and-a-half point long pole into its repertoire of weapons.

Who were these two men? Who were their respective teachers—Leung Lan Kwai and the Abbot Chi Shin? How did Leung Jan come to learn from them? At this juncture historical records begin to fade away, even as legend and oral history begin to take over. To make matters worse, Wing Chun's connection with rebels seeking to "overthrow the Qing [empire] and restore the Ming" means that its own practitioners deliberately obfuscated the truth about its origins. In Leung Jan's time and before, Wing Chun practitioners seem to have invented stories to throw people off the scent, to downplay the effectiveness of the art and in some cases to get rid of people who were asking silly questions. Ip Man and Wong Shung Leung would repeat this pattern even in modern times (see below).

To appreciate just how unclear the origins of Wing Chun are before Leung Jan's time, one need only point out that the Shaolin Temple mentioned in these accounts is often the Southern Shaolin Temple in Fujian, not the Northern Shaolin Temple in Henan province that most people imagine. Even modern Wing Chun instructors have confused the two. And yet there is much dispute about whether a Southern Temple even existed, let alone where it was located. The current Abbott of the Northern Shaolin Temple, Abbott Shi Yongxin, has reportedly said, "In all the records of the Shaolin Monastery, I have never seen the words 'Southern Shaolin.'"[4] This appears to contradict the countless references to the Southern Shaolin Temple in the folklore and oral history of the South. It is known that the Qing crushed a rebellion in Fujian, that there is a town in Fujian province called "Eternal Spring"

---

4. https://en.wikipedia.org/wiki/Southern_Shaolin_Monastery#Controversy 300816 quoting: "在我們少林寺所有的典籍中,我從來沒有看到過『南少林』的字樣."

(pronounced "wing chun" in the local dialect), and that Ip Man may have mentioned the origins of his art as stemming from Fujian.

Unraveling complicated threads of contradictory accounts dating back more than two hundred years ago is no simple task. To understand Wing Chun's origins from earlier than the 1800s is to try and fathom events that took place in a world very different from our own, where people's practice of Wing Chun combined with their opposition to tyranny posed a danger to their lives and meant the difference between liberty or death.

Some say Leung Jan was apprenticed to the Red Boat Opera company where he met Leung Yee Tai and Wong Wah Bo. Others say the two men came to Leung's father for medical treatment and eventually agreed to pass on their skills to his son. Perhaps this was their way of thanking Leung's father for treating them at his clinic free of charge. Perhaps the "Apricot Tea Hall" was a place where anti-Qing rebels could seek out free medical treatment to heal their wounds or exchange information. Perhaps Leung's father was an anti-Qing sympathizer. But all this is conjecture, and perhaps we will never know the truth.

And so begin the folktales and myths surrounding the origins of this art. The most popular account of this story begins at the Shaolin Temple (though of course it is not clear which Shaolin Temple is meant). The Shaolin Temple was harboring anti-Qing rebels. Perhaps it was even training them. The Qing Emperor tracked them down and destroyed the temple, but some of the monks escaped.

One of these fugitives was the nun Ng Mei—an expert martial artist. On the run from the Qing authorities in the 1700s, Ng Mei fled to the Dalian mountains. There she continued refining her martial arts practice. One day she came across a crane and snake fighting. Observing their movements closely, she further refined her own fighting techniques. One day she was in town buying bean curd from her favorite tofu vendor, Yim Yee. Yim mentioned how a local warlord was harassing his daughter, Wing Chun, insisting that she marry him. Ng Mei took pity on Yim Yee and began teaching his daughter her fighting skills. Wing Chun fended off the warlord by challenging him to a fight on condition that if she defeated him, he would leave her in peace. Needless to say, Wing Chun gave him a sound beating and saved herself from the forced marriage. Later she went on to marry Leung Bok Chau and taught him the fighting skills she had learnt from the nun Ng Mei. Both of them went on to teach others. Leung Bok Chau named the style after his wife, Wing Chun. Eventually this art came to Leun Lan Kwai who taught it to Wang Wah Bo (the anti-Qing opera actor who passed it on to Leung Jan at the herbal clinic in Foshan). Meanwhile, Leung Yee Tai had learnt the pole technique from Abbot Shi Chin who had, like Ng Mei, also survived the Qing attack on the Shaolin Temple. Perhaps the Abbot had also taken refuge on the Red Boat opera.

Sifu Loukas and other students at the now-legendary London Wing Chun school known as "The Basement" recall a lecture given in 1987 by Sifu Wong Shun Leung (one of Ip Man's most respected senior students):

> *My grandmaster Wong Shun Leung pointed out that the story of Ng Mei had been made up by a disciple of Grandmaster Ip Man who was a journalist. He wanted to raise the profile of Wing Chun which at that time was not very well known in Hong Kong.*

Others recall that once a journalist suggested "All Chinese martial arts are based on animal styles. So what animal style is Wing Chun based on?" The implication in the question was obvious: if Wing Chun is a respectable Chinese martial art how come it's not based on an animal? In response to this ridiculous question Ip Man replied: "Crane and Snake," or "Monkey and Snake." They all had a good laugh about it afterwards. As Sifu Loukas likes to tell his students, "Wing Chun teaches us how to respond to stupid questions with intelligent answers."

Recorded history from this time does, however, give us some interesting clues. Almost all the different branches of Wing Chun trace their origins to the Red Boat Opera troupe operating on the Pearl River Delta near Foshan. So we can be pretty sure that Wing Chun was connected to the activities of the Red Boat Opera. Fortunately the history of Cantonese opera is fairly well preserved. And for Wing Chun practitioners it makes interesting reading:

> *In the Qing dynasty (1644–1911) one man, Cheung Ng (1720 AD) a northern opera actor, had a great influenced [sic] on present-day Yuet Kahk [Cantonese Opera]. Escaping authorities due to his anti-Manchu activities, he fled southwards to Canton. Hiding out amongst Cantonese opera troupes he taught and passed the knowledge of performing the traditional "Eighteen plays of Cantonese Opera." His contributions earned him a place in Taoist opera heaven, where he, along with the god of Chinese Opera "Waih Gong," is worshiped by "Disciples of the Pear Garden" at every performance.[5]*

Cheung Ng was not only famous for his skills in the opera. He was well known as an accomplished martial artist and, of course, an anti-Qing rebel. He was soon given the nickname "Tan-sau Ng." Was this a reference to his Wing Chun skills and his unstoppable tan-sau palm?

The Cantonese opera groups were clearly regarded with suspicion by the Qing authorities. A full-fledged rebellion broke out in 1844:

> *An opera performer, Lee Mun Mou (李文茂), a member of a notorious anti-Manchu group [the Qing were sometimes called "Manchus" because they came from Manchuria], led his and other opera troupes into an uprising against the Manchu government at the same time as the Taiping Tianguo Christian uprising (1844 AD). They dressed*

---

5. http://www.lifeofguangzhou.com/node_10/node_228/node_233/node_241/2006/01/25/1138175 70033.shtml 110814.

in full operatic costumes and using the martial arts they acquired in their operatic training fought the Manchu to no avail.

Performing Yuet Kahk was banned all together in the mid Qing dynasty (1855 AD) after this incident. Performers involved in the uprising or associated with Lee Mun Mou were killed by the hundreds. Those whether if they were involved in the uprising or not, were disallowed to perform their art. A Manchurian attempt to stop the ever so present Cantonese independent identity. Cantonese opera troupes disbanded and members not knowing any other lifestyle went to other provinces...[6]

We know that Dr. Leung Jan began studying Wing Chun in or around the 1850s. It seems likely that the Red Boat Opera was set up as a front for anti-Qing rebels and that they were actively engaged in plotting a major rebellion. Anyone who has studied Wing Chun knows that it is far too sophisticated and technical an art to have been invented by one person in a short period of time. It is far more likely that the martial artists hiding out with the Cantonese opera companies continued training, exchanging notes, and refining their skills by practicing together as well as engaging with Qing officers in real-life encounters. Interestingly, Jin Young, a contemporary Brazilian Ju-Jitsu practitioner who says Wing Chun has improved his grappling, summed up the genius of Wing Chun as follows:

Imagine if you took the greatest living masters of different styles and put them all in one room. You gave them a pencil and paper and said: "You can only leave this room once you have written down on the paper all the concepts you agree on that would work in a real-life combat situation. If even one of you disagrees, you cannot write it down. You can only write down the principles, not the techniques, that you agree are the most important in a real-life situation for a martial artist to keep in mind. For example: "the shortest distance for an attack is a straight line. If you agree you write it down." In the end ... when you opened the door and looked at that paper, it would be a summary of the concepts of Wing Chun...[7]

It is not inconceivable that some of the injured fighters from the Cantonese opera rebellion sought medical aid at Leung Jan's father's herbal clinic in Foshan. They would not have been able to pay for their treatment. The historical reference to the Apricot Forest and the folk-hero Teng Weng's free treatment of the poor suggests that Leung Jan's father treated some patients for free. And when the Qing suppressed the rebellion and finally banned the opera troupes in 1855, Wang Wah Bo and Leung Yee Tai may have decided to repay Leung's father's generosity by passing their skills on to his son.

Wing Chun is a martial art that demands honesty from its practitioners. In the end the most honest thing we can say about its origin before Dr. Leung Jan in Foshan in the 1850s is

---

6. Ibid.
7. https://www.youtube.com/watch?v=5PGS61EwnpU 300816

that we cannot be sure about it, and perhaps never will be. Ng Mei, according to some accounts, is a fictional character from popular folktales.

But Leung Jan must have been a kindly person. The folktales and movies surrounding his exploits—half fictional or completely fictional accounts—are testimony to his popularity in Foshan. According to some accounts Dr. Leung remained undefeated in over three hundred challenge matches against martial artists from all sorts of different styles. However, Dr. Leung only taught his skills to a handful of select students—among them were his neighbor Money-Changer Wah, and his own sons, Leung Bik and Leung Chan.

*

Not much is known about Ip Man's training with Ng Jung So (the senior student old Money-Changer Wah put in charge to teach Ip Man after his death). It has been suggested that Ng Jung So is somewhat of an unsung hero in the Wing Chun lineage and this is probably true. In any case Ip Man was only to train with him for about two years until he was fifteen years old. After that he was sent to Hong Kong to study at St. Stephen's College.

While in Hong Kong, Ip Man was introduced to an old Kung-fu fighter who turned out to be none other than Leung Bik—Dr. Leung Jan's son! Unlike Money-Changer Wah, Leung Bik was well educated and could explain the theoretical and technical aspects of Wing Chun in a way that Money-Changer Wah could not. Of course Ip Man was somewhat older now and perhaps mature enough to learn from Leung Bik what he was unable to grasp from Chan Wah-Shun in his childhood. It is worthwhile remembering that Dr. Leung Jan was a medical expert and would have been well versed in traditional Chinese theories of medicine that include knowledge of qi and human anatomy. Perhaps the lettered Leung Bik was able to teach Ip Man the subtleties of Wing Chun that he had not picked up in his younger days in Foshan.

Ip Man trained with Leung Bik for about four years and completed his studies at St. Stephen's. It seems he had had plans to continue his studies in Kobe in Japan. But it was 1914. War was declared in Europe and the world would forever be changed. Japan declared war on Germany and seized German fortresses in China. In 1917, China would join the Allies and pay a heavy price for it.

For the next twenty years Ip Man worked in the army and police force. All the while China suffered one tragedy after another. In 1919, the Allies signed the treaty of Versailles ending the First World War. However, the treaty gave Japan possessions in China. This outraged the Chinese—who had once again been humiliated and betrayed by the Europeans. China refused to sign the treaty and in 1918 a group called the "Society for the Study of Marxism" was formed in Beijing. And so the seeds of communism were planted on Chinese soil.

During these turbulent times Ip Man practiced Wing Chun with his peers at his residence in Foshan. It must have been a rare pleasure to be able to exchange notes on Kung-fu with friends, to continue the process of self-discovery that Wing Chun unleashes in all its practitioners, and to preserve a precious Chinese tradition in a time when so much in Chinese society was vulnerable and under attack. But the worst was yet to come.

> *Between 1920–25 there was anarchy among disputing war lords in China and many anti-foreign incidents. The Chinese Communist Party came into being. Sun Yat-sen died and Chiang K'ai-shek rose to power as leader of the Kuomintang (the Nationalists).*[8]

The Nationalists and Communists began fighting each other and then, in 1937, Japan invaded China. Ip Man refused to cooperate with the occupying Japanese forces, and so had to suffer the consequences. This could not have been an easy decision: Ip Man was married and had four children. Because of his principles he had to give up his job and his family's property. And so it was not long before he had fallen into poverty. But Wing Chun came to Ip Man's rescue. When a close friend began supporting Ip financially, he repaid the favor by teaching his son. He also began teaching at the Luen Cheung Cotton Mill between 1941 and 1943.

*

> *In August 1945 the Americans dropped atomic bombs on [the Japanese cities of] Hiroshima and Nagasaki. The Russians invaded Manchuria; the Japanese surrendered… In China a full-scale civil war between Communists led by Mao Tse-tung and Nationalists under Chiang K'ai-shek … ended in victory for Mao's forces and [the] Chinese People's Republic was established.*[9]

Fortunately most of us can only imagine what the aftermath of war must feel like. Ip Man was now in his fifties. Born just after the Boxer Rebellion, he had witnessed the occupation of China by foreign forces; seen first hand the destructive effects of English opium trafficking on Chinese life; and experienced the racism and prejudice of Westerners, the looting and raping of the Japanese, the plunder and pillaging of outsiders, and the reckless self-destruction of the Chinese in their own civil war. Born into wealth and prestige in a China that still proudly recalled its glorious past, he lived through the turmoil and chaos of a new China emerging, one that would react to all the foreign led destruction of China, by turning in upon itself and destroying much of what was left of the old ways. Under Communism the old Chinese cultures, traditions, and customs were frowned upon and seen as decadent. The new China had turned its back on the glorious past.

---

8. Pat Barr, *Foreign Devils: Westerners in the Far East. The Sixteenth Century to the Present Day* (Harmondsworth: Penguin Books, 1970), 87.
9. Ibid.

But the martial arts were a part of that past that could not easily be destroyed. It is easy to imagine how Ip Man's Wing Chun would have helped him cope with the difficulties of all those years. "Wing Chun teaches us how to manage under pressure," says Sifu Loukas. Many of Loukas's students point out that they have become better people because of their Wing Chun—they can cope with difficult situations by not panicking. They keep their calm, maintain their focus, accept the situation, and then deal with things appropriately. There is little doubt that Wing Chun would have been a solid support in Ip Man's life at this time. As he continued his own personal practice of this rich tradition that began so long ago that its origins are lost in myth, and as he continued to refine his understanding of the art that was passed on to him from Leung Bik, Money-Changer Wah, and Ng Chung So, Ip Man could not have known that one day this treasure of the Chinese would be respected and preserved by people from all over the world. And he himself would become a legend.

The Qing had been overthrown—they were now just a name from the past. But the Ming could not be restored since they no longer existed. China had awoken into the modern world. But it was not the China of fable. And yet Ip Man had brought with him something out of that past that was fabulous and profound and worthy of respect. Wing Chun practitioners would no longer belong to secret societies seeking to overthrow tyrant emperors. They would now belong to very open communities of practitioners for whom Wing Chun would continue to enrich their lives, and who, for their part, could continue to enrich that tradition by becoming a part of it and contributing their own discoveries to it.

And so begins a new phase in the history of Wing Chun.

3
GROWING AND CONTINUING
Two Legendary Students of Grandmaster Ip Man

February 1, 1954. Ip Man has been in Hong Kong for the last four years. The British colony has changed considerably since he was last here as a student. But Ip Man has changed too—he is now around sixty-years old. He has lived through several wars, foreign occupation, and revolution. And of course he is an accomplished master of Wing Chun.

Through the introduction of a friend, he has been teaching Wing Chun to members of the Restaurant Workers' Union at Hoi Tan Road in Kowloon. Initially there are only a few students but the numbers have been growing slowly. Today is a particularly quiet night. Tomorrow is Chinese New Year's Eve and most people have other things to do. Suddenly a young lad walks into the school. His cousin has told him there is a sifu here who teaches a form of boxing from Foshan in Guangdong province. The young man has witnessed some of this teacher's students in a challenge match, and he liked what he saw. He wants to know how good these students really are.

To everyone's surprise the young man asks if he can spar with one of Ip Man's students. Is this a challenge? As always, Ip Man is calm and polite. The young man spars with the first student and makes short work of him. Ip Man asks him to cross hands with another student. Again the young man defeats him easily. "Why don't we play together?" says Ip Man.

And so the old Ip Man and the young upstart touch hands. The young man has obviously studied boxing. He launches punches at Ip Man, but the old man hardly seems to move. As the young lad moves around and launches another attack, Ip Man steps forward, forcing him against the wall. The lad suddenly finds his hands pinned at the elbow while the old man launches a burst of light punches at his head and chest.

But the young lad is not deterred. He tries again—now skipping lightly on his feet, bobbing and weaving, jabbing to the right, hooking with the left. But again Ip Man pins his arms effortlessly and launches a shower of light punches. Enough? Not yet. The young upstart steps back. Perhaps he launches a few kicks; perhaps he tries a feint. But the end is still the same: the old man has him up against the wall. And the punches come flying in.

There are slightly different versions of this encounter. But what's clear is that the young man has found the teacher he's been looking for.

'What's your name?" asks Ip Man.

The young man looks into the old man's eyes. "Wong Shun Leung."

*

Wong Shun Leung was nineteen years old when he met Ip Man and became his student. His father had been an accomplished doctor in Guangdong province before moving to Hong Kong where Wong Shun Leung was born in 1935. Like Ip Man, Wong's father had grown up to see China emerge from a colonial past and two world wars into a modern, Communist state. And Wong had tasted something of the bitterness of foreign invasion and occupation himself, having grown up during the Second World War. These experiences combined with a solid education and the unique responsibilities that come from being the eldest surviving son in a family of eight children, most of whom were girls, produced in Wong a strong sense of chivalry and fair play. He also had a powerful aversion to tall tales and little tolerance for nonsense. He developed in the end a personality that sought deeper meaning through the pursuit of excellence. In a sense, though it may be a cliché to say this, Wong seemed to be seeking "truth" through his study of the martial arts.

And that study led him to explore different styles of fighting and to test them out in real conflicts. On one occasion he overheard his Wu-Style Tai Chi teacher claim he had witnessed an old Kung-fu master stop a moving car by generating chi through his palms. Apparently Wong collected his belongings and walked out without saying a word. He never returned to that teacher again.

On another occasion he knocked out his boxing instructor during a sparring session. The instructor tried to exact revenge the following day, leaving Wong no choice but to continue his search for a genuine teacher elsewhere. By the time he met Ip Man, Wong was already a capable boxer with fighting experience. He had also learned Tai Chi and so understood the feeling of energy (chi) that comes from correct posture and body-alignment. This put him in good stead to learn the more subtle aspects of Wing Chun, which otherwise elude the practitioner.

Ip Man saw talent and determination in his young student: "Look at how he hits the wall bag," he once remarked to another student as Wong pounded away with lightning-fast fists. "He punches like he's hitting a real person. You watch this lad. He's going to stir up a storm in Hong Kong…"

Ip Man was right. Wong Shun Leung wanted to test the new discoveries he was making. And Ip Man encouraged him to do so. In a short time Wong had had almost a hundred challenge fights (beimo) and remained undefeated. His exploits became famous all over Hong Kong, and his contests were reported in newspapers and magazines.

From the 1960s onwards Wong would invite specific Wing Chun practitioners to his home on Nathan Road. At first these sessions were simply a means of testing his own skills and refining his own knowledge of Wing Chun. He did not consider himself a teacher. A number of Ip Man's students would visit Wong to further enhance their training. They were all students of Ip Man, and Wong would not let them call him sifu. So they would call him *Leung Goh* —"Elder Brother Leung"—instead.

Finally, in 1969, Wong Shun Leung officially opened a school of Wing Chun. By this time, his own teacher, Grandmaster Ip Man was in his late seventies and was semi-retired. Ip Man would pass away three years later.

Wong Shun Leung was instrumental in making the relatively unknown style of Wing Chun famous all over Hong Kong, and he remains to this day one of Ip Man's most revered students.

*

Also living in Nathan Road at the time was the son of a Cantonese opera actor who had been born in San Francisco in 1940. The circumstances of his birth, as well as those of his death, are often surrounded by superstition even to this day:

> *Hoi Cheun and Grace Li felt their children were locked under the unkind eyes of the spirits. Their first child—a boy—died shortly after birth, a bad omen. According to Chinese beliefs, the loss of a son is much worse than the loss of a baby girl. When Grace became pregnant a second time, she feared yet another dark moment.*
>
> *Knowing the second child in a Chinese family should be a girl, the couple adopted a daughter named Phoebe to confuse the spirits. A few months later, Grace gave birth to a healthy boy, Peter. In 1940, a third boy—Grace's second living biological child—was born. Again hoping to fool the spirits, Grace gave the baby a girl's name, Sai Fon (which means "Small Phoenix") and pierced one of his ears. She soon renamed the boy Jun Fan, or "Return Again," because she felt he would one day return to his birthplace. But it was the doctor, Mary Glover, who nicknamed the child "Bruce"—the name that stuck. He later Americanized his family name to Lee.[10]*

Bruce Lee was destined to become the man who would bring Chinese Kung-fu to the attention of the world. But as a child growing up in Hong Kong in the 1950s, that destiny was far from obvious:

> *Although Bruce Lee was part of a wealthy family and had the opportunity to attend fine private schools, he was drawn to the rough and ragged crowds of the streets. He eventually formed his own street gang, the Tigers of Junction Street. From time to time, Bruce and the Tigers finished on the losing side of a fight. Bruised and bleeding, Bruce would storm home, demanding to be trained in martial arts so he could defend himself. Eventually, his father showed him some Tai Chi, but the slow-flowing movements of this type of martial art offered little help in a street fight. ... Besides, it takes*

---

10. Rachel A. Koestler-Grack, *Bruce Lee* (New York, NY: Chelsea House, 2007), 11–12.

decades of practice before Tai Chi can be used as an effective fighting tool, and Bruce had no patience for that.

Still, Bruce sometimes went with his father to Tai Chi lessons. "I got tired of it quickly," Bruce later confessed in M. Uyehara's Bruce Lee: Incomparable Fighter. "It was no fun for a kid. Just a bunch of old men." On one occasion, he hurt a Tai Chi instructor on purpose.

He was fifteen at the time and had already started training in another martial arts form. The teacher often put on demonstrations to prove his strength, calling up volunteers to punch him in the stomach. One after another, members of the audience tried to hurt the old man but failed. Finally, Bruce raised his hand and went up. The old man smiled and exposed his stomach. As hard as he could, Bruce deliberately thrust his right hand into the instructor's ribs. There was a quick crack, and the man crumbled to the floor moaning. Obviously unimpressed by Tai Chi, Bruce went searching for a fighting form that would prove useful.[11]

Bruce Lee had already found the "useful fighting form" he was looking for when he was introduced to Ip Man's Wing Chun. He was, interestingly enough, thirteen years old at the time. Perhaps he reminded Ip Man of his own childhood days in Foshan, when he had approached the aging Chan Wah Shun at about the same age. Bruce Lee would, of course, go on to inspire generations of Chinese Kung-fu enthusiasts. But before that time he still had a lot to learn. Least of all, he had to be taught how to control his impetuousness and stay out of trouble.

It is easy to understand how Wing Chun would have ultimately been a calming influence on Bruce Lee's life. All Wing Chun practitioners come to realize that they need to remain calm in the face of pressure, that they need to keep cool when taunted, and that they need to respond intelligently and naturally to aggressive people. Although in the beginning Bruce Lee was keen to try out the day's Wing Chun lesson on the Hong Kong streets, and he had a reputation for being "fighting crazy," it is clear to the careful observer that over time Wing Chun practice would become a stabilizing force in his life. An interesting clue about the nature of this change is the fact that a year after starting Wing Chun training, Bruce also took up Cha-Cha dance lessons: he was starting to proactively take charge of his life, rather than simply hanging out with the street gangs trying to impress girls.

But Bruce Lee's popularity, his boisterous nature, his almost-arrogant self-confidence, and his unpleasant habit of using too much force on his fellow students started to take its toll. Some of the students at the Restaurant Workers Union were not happy with his attitude. Word got out that Bruce Lee had German ancestry and so was of mixed race. Ip Man may have had mixed feelings about teaching foreigners. After all that his generation had suffered,

---

11. Ibid. 22–23.

this was hardly surprising. And now people began to pressure him to stop teaching Bruce Lee because he was not "purely" Chinese.

Just as Ip Man's own teacher put Ng Chung So in charge of teaching him, so Ip Man sent Bruce Lee to Wong Shung Leung to continue his Wing Chun training, telling Wong that the boy had talent. Ip Man clearly liked Bruce Lee, despite what others said about him, and he sent him to one of his best students. Wong would prove to be an excellent mentor and very quickly they would become lifelong friends. Later in life, Wong Shun Leung would recall the first time he was introduced to Bruce Lee, describing him as an "Elvis-like character.":

> *One day, about twenty years ago, I practiced my Kung-fu in Master Ip's institute. I also helped my fellow learners in their practice. At that time, Chang brought in an Elvis-like youngster. He leaned his body to one side with his hand on the wall. The other hand was in the back pocket of his trousers. His body was supported by one of his legs only. He swayed his body continuously. His manner was very frivolous as though he thought that he was smart. I really did not like his appearance. After he went away, I told Chang that I did not welcome this young man.*
>
> *A few months later, he came for the second time. This time, he dressed properly and was more polite. Master Ip liked him very much, so he took him to be his disciple. He immediately came over and greeted me. This was so sudden that I just could not understand. We became fellow learners and friends. From then on, he brought me a lot of trouble. That young man was Bruce Lee, the famous international star.* [12]

"The trouble" that Bruce Lee brought to Wong was the result of his constant desire to want to test his abilities in street fights. In one sense he was just following the example set by Wong Shung Leung and other Wing Chun practitioners who had become somewhat notorious for participating in beimo fights to test their skills against other martial artists. But for Bruce Lee's generation the niceties and protocols of the older generations were missing. Whereas the older martial artists were perhaps more interested in testing the virtue of their school by crossing hands with practitioners from other schools in semi-friendly challenge matches, the younger generation of Hong Kong martial arts students were much more interested in proving their personal fighting superiority over their peers. There was also an intense need to feel safe from the violence of others. The Hong Kong of Bruce Lee's youth seemed to be a violent place. As ordinary people everywhere struggled to make a living, young people without many options naturally gravitated to groups that gave them a sense of control and purpose. For some this meant gang culture. Much later in his life Bruce Lee would reflect on how this environment encouraged him to learn to fight to protect himself:

---

12. Attributed to Wong Shun Leung at http://www.wongvingtsun.co.uk/articles.htm 130814.

> *Being a skinny kid, Bruce reminisced, "I always fought with my gang behind me. In school, our favorite weapon was the chains we'd find in the cans (toilets). Those days, kids improvised all kinds of weapons—even shoes with razors attached.*
> *"I only took up Kung-fu [...] when I began to feel insecure. I kept wondering what would happen to me if my gang was not around when I met a rival gang."*[13]

But there was much more to the young Bruce Lee than just fear of violence. He seemed to have a burning desire to constantly improve himself—a theme that would describe his entire life and explains why he was not content to simply learn Wing Chun but to constantly test his abilities in situations that would allow him room for further growth and excellence.

On one occasion, in 1958, Bruce wanted to test his abilities in an inter-school boxing match. Wong encouraged him, saying that it was important to get as much combat experience as possible in order to improve as a martial artist, and he agreed to coach him in the rules of Western boxing alongside his Wing Chun. With Wong Shun Leung in his corner, Bruce began the first round of the boxing match in a Wing Chung fighting stance that immediately brought jeers from the crowd. But their voices were quickly silenced as Bruce Lee swiftly knocked down his opponent—the reigning champion—in the very first round. Later, conflicting accounts of this contest would say that Lee won on points—combining Western boxing techniques with the lightning-fast punches of Wing Chun that left his opponent unable to counterattack. Either way, it is clear that Bruce Lee's victory was decisive and uncontested. And that a skinny Chinese kid from St Francis Xavier school had beaten one of King George V School's best boxers. King George V was a predominantly British expatriate school with a strong record in the Inter-School Boxing Championships. The King George boys were also sworn enemies of the mostly local Chinese boys from St Francis Xavier. Bruce Lee was the only fighter to bring home a victory for his school that night. It must have felt good. And Wing Chun had given him the edge. In that same year Lee also won Hong Kong's Crown Colony Cha-Cha Championships.

Such victories gave Lee a new sense of confidence—not only in himself but also in Wing Chun's effectiveness. Before he took up Wing Chun, Bruce Lee's life had been characterized by failures at school, street fighting, and getting into trouble with the police. The practice of Wing Chun under Wong Shun Leung enabled him to prove to himself and to others that he could be successful not only in combat but in other things too. His superb talent for Cha-Cha dancing enhanced his prestige, won him some fame, and in turn complemented his practice of Wing Chun. Life seemed to be improving.

Lee began improvising in his training—taking what he learnt from western boxing, and from dancing, and transferring it to his practice of Wing Chun. And taking the principles of Wing Chun and transferring those ideas to his dancing, and to life in general. He used contraptions such as steel bars with weighs to strengthen his arms and improve the speed of his

---

13. M. Uyehara, *Bruce Lee: The Incomparable Fighter* (Burbank: Ohara Publications, 1977), 7.

punches. Where before he might have used anger, outrage, insults, and violence to confront his enemies, now he used wit, charm, and cunning. As all Wing Chun practitioners know, the most efficient way to gain victory is not to fight force with force, but to be like water—and flow between the forces of your opponents, taking the obstacle as the way. In this formative period of his life, the early foundations of a new structure were being built deep within his psyche. And they would emerge years later in spectacular fashion, propelling him to a fame and influence beyond the wildest imaginations of anyone who knew him then.

But while all of this was brewing deep within, on the outside he was still up to his old tricks. On one occasion he intercepted his fellow students before they could get to their class with Wong Shun Leung. Telling them that the class was cancelled, he sent them away, even going so far as to escort one of his friends back to the bus stop and waiving him good bye as he got onto the bus heading back home. He then ran back to Wong Shun Leung's place to enjoy a private lesson with his teacher. Wong Shun Leung was puzzled why no other students had arrived. Bruce Lee put it down to their lack of enthusiasm, saying that Wong Sun Leung shouldn't bother to teach those lazy guys.

More seriously, however, he ended up getting into a fight with the son of a triad gang member. The triads were organized criminal families that were feared in Hong Kong society and even intimidated the police. The local police chief visited Lee's father and told him that he would not be able to keep overlooking his son's behavior and that this time Lee had gone too far and had messed with the wrong crowd. Finally, for his own safety, and in a desperate final attempt to try to make something of his son, Bruce Lee's father decided to send him overseas—to the USA. Perhaps there he would make something of himself, learning life's most important lessons the hard way.

In 1959, Bruce Lee bade farewell to his family and headed off to America—to San Francisco—the place of his birth. From there he moved to Seattle where his father had arranged for him to live under the strict discipline of Ruby Chow. Chow's husband was an old friend and colleague of Lee's father. His wife owned a restaurant in China Town and was known to be a tough boss. Lee would live in a small room above her restaurant and work in the kitchen during the day. He could also pursue his studies and try to make something of himself the old-fashioned way—with hard work and tough love.

The fact is that Lee always wanted to make something of himself. A careful look at his childhood in Hong Kong shows that he always wanted to be more than just average. In the youth culture of the Hong Kong streets that meant being a gang leader and winning fights. That's why Bruce Lee insisted on learning Kung-fu—to be a better fighter. In Wing Chun he began to see a system of Chinese martial arts that actually allowed a smaller, "weaker" person to overcome a "stronger," bigger opponent. But also in Wing Chun he discovered principles that became a foundation for all of his life-long pursuits: he could set himself a goal, build strong foundations, and pursue that goal relentlessly using every obstacle as an opportunity to find the way. And in America there were plenty of ways to make something of yourself: the most successful and celebrated Americans were movie stars. Acting was in his blood. As a child—through his father's connections—he had even made a few appearances in Hong Kong movies. Part of the genius of Bruce Lee was that he combined all the things he loved—not fighting as such, but the science of fighting first revealed to him in Wing Chun; expressing the human body through choreography and dance; telling stories, charming others, being creative and "looking good." In America he also discovered a deep interest in Eastern and Western philosophy, met the woman he would marry, raised a family, and became an international superstar.

In the end he would forge his own style of fighting—deeply indebted to Wing Chun principles—but not beholden to any one tradition. And he would return to Hong Kong, in the 1970s, to a crowd of cheering fans greeting him at the airport and asking him for his autograph. There is a lot more to the Bruce Lee story. But there is little doubt that he single handedly contributed to making Chinese Kung-fu, Chinese movies, Chinese culture, and Wing Chun itself famous and respected throughout the world. He also helped revolutionize approaches to fight cinematography and inspired generations of young people after him to pursue excellence through the study of martial arts. In a now-famous interview with Pierre Berton in 1971 he summarized his philosophy in these iconic words first spoken by one of his TV characters, words that are also a beautiful expression of Wing Chun's approach to fighting:

> *Empty your mind, be formless, shapeless, like water. Now you put water into a cup, it becomes the cup. You put water into a bottle, it becomes the bottle. You put it in a teapot, it becomes the teapot. Now water can flow, or it can crash! Be water, my friend.*[14]

Bruce Lee died under mysterious circumstances on July 20, 1973, at the height of his career and the peak of his physical strength. Although there are many theories about his death, it may well be that it was simply the result of heat stroke exacerbated by Lee's overtraining, the fact that he had had his underarm sweat glands removed, and the hot Hong Kong weather on the day he died. According to Matthew Polly who proposed this theory in his 2018 biography of Lee, heat stroke among athletes was poorly understood at the time but is now recognized as a cause of death among elite sportspeople.[15] Among Bruce Lee's many great legacies was the founding of his own philosophy of martial arts that he named Jeet Kune Do—Way of the Intercepting Fist.

Before his untimely death he did have an opportunity to meet up with his old master, Ip Man, and even engaged in a friendly sparring match with Wong Shun Leung. In a visit to Ip Man he exchanged ideas about fighting, showed up the poor technique in some of those very

---

14. The show ran on Canadian TV from 1962 to 1973. Berton regularly interviewed important artists, actors, and public figures including Malcolm X. The quote is from his interview with Bruce Lee on December 9, 1971.
15. Matthew Polly, *Bruce Lee: A Life* (New York, NY: Simon & Schuster, 2018), ch. 25.

same senior students who had discouraged Ip Man from teaching him when he was a teenager, and impressed and delighted his old teacher. By this time Bruce Lee was already famous and successful as a martial-arts movie star. His outspoken criticism of blind adherence to what he called "dead forms," combined with deliberately provocative and misleading newspaper stories stirred up jealousy among some of those old Kung-fu seniors who accused him of disrespecting Wing Chun. To put these rumors to rest and set the record straight, the old master and the young movie star, who Ip Man had always referred to affectionately as "Upstart," went out for afternoon tea:

> *The truth was Bruce respected Ip Man, and Ip Man liked Up-start. Whatever larger critique he was making in public, Bruce was extremely polite and solicitous to Ip Man in person. Whatever reservations Ip Man may have felt about Bruce's public remarks about traditional Kung-fu, he was clever enough to appreciate that having the most famous martial arts actor in Asia as one of his disciples was a net positive for him. To quash rumors of a rift, Bruce invited Ip Man out for yum cha (afternoon tea and dim sum) at a restaurant near Kowloon Park. While they ate, Bruce smiled at Ip Man and asked, "Do you still treat me as your student?"*
>
> *Ip Man quickly replied, "Do you still treat me as your sifu?" Both men laughed.*
>
> *After they were done, Bruce said, "Sifu, we haven't gone for a walk together in a long time. How about we take a walk?" They strolled along the very busy Nathan Road so the public could see that their relationship was good.*[16]

Ip man himself passed away on December 2nd, 1972. Bruce Lee never made it to his funeral—none of Ip Man's students informed Bruce Lee of his death and one of them even prevented his son from calling Lee—a fact which they later admitted, and for which Bruce Lee never forgave them.[17] Despite what some people say, both Wong Shun Leung and Ip Man remained dear to Bruce Lee. In a letter he wrote to Wong Shun Leung in 1970 he clearly expresses his affection and gratitude to his old teacher and mentor, thanking Ip Man and Wong Shun Leung for not only teaching him the fighting skills of Wing Chun but also practical principles for success in life.

---

16. Matthew Polly, *Bruce Lee: A Life* (New York, NY: Simon & Schuster, 2018), 532.
17. Ibid. 534.

A Letter from Bruce Lee to Wong Shun Leung

Dear Shun-Leung, January 11, 1970

It has been a long time since I last wrote to you. How are you? Alan Shaw's letter from Canada asks me to lend you my 8mm film. I am sorry about that. It is because I have lost it when I moved my home. That film is already very old and I seldom use it, so I have lost it. I am sorry for it.

Now I have bought a house in Bel-Air. It is about half an acre. There are many trees. It has the taste of a range. It is located on a hilltop near Beverly Hills. Moreover, besides my son Brandon, I have had a daughter, Shannon, who is seven months old now. Have you re-married? Please send my regards to your sisters.

Recently, I have organized a film production company. I have also written a story "The Silent Flute." James Coburn and I will act in it. Stirling Silliphant is the screen-play writer. He is a famous screen-play writer *(In the Heat of the Night)*. We plan to make the first fighting film in Hollywood. The prospect is good. About six months later, the filming work will begin. All who participate in this film are my followers. In the future, Steve McQueen may also work together with me. I am very excited about this plan.

As to martial art, I still practice daily. I teach my students and friends twice a week. It doesn't matter if they are Western boxers, taekwondo practitioners, or wrestlers, I will teach them as long as they are friendly and will not get uptight.

Since I started to practice realistically in 1966 (protectors, gloves, etc.), I feel that I had many prejudices before, and they are wrong. So I change the name of the gist of my study to Jeet Kune Do. Jeet Kune Do is only a name. The most important thing is to avoid having bias in the training. Of course, I run every day, I practice my tools (punch, kick, throw, etc.). I have to raise the basic conditions daily. Although the principle of boxing is important, practicality is even more important.

I thank you and Master [Ip Man] for teaching me the ways of Wing Chun in Hong Kong. Actually, I have to thank you for leading me to walk on a practical road. Especially in the States, there are Western boxers, I often practice with them, too. There are many so-called masters in Wing Chun here, I really hope that they will not be so blind to fight with those Western boxers!

I may make a trip to Hong Kong. I hope that you are still living in the same place. We are intimate friends, we need to meet more and chat about our past days. That will be a lot of fun, don't you think? When you see Master Ip, please send my regard to him. Happiness be with you!

Bruce Lee.[18]

---

18. John Little, ed., *Letters of the Dragon: An Anthology of Bruce Lee's Correspondence with Family, Friends, and Fans 1958–1973*, 2nd ed. (Tokyo: Tuttle Publishing, 2016), 162.

4
IN THE PRESENT AND ON TO THE FUTURE
From Sifu Wong Shun Leung to Sifu Loukas Kastrounis

Undeniably, Bruce Lee was the most spectacular of Wong Shun Leung's students. But Sifu Wong had many other students too who would go on to promote Wing Chun in their own unique ways. In the early 1970s a young musician working at the Hong Kong Sheraton Hotel by the name of Nino Bernardo discovered that some of the counterattacks his boxing coach had taught him came from Wing Chun Kung-fu. A colleague at the Sheraton used to visit a monk to learn energy techniques to help him with his breathing. Nino asked his colleague to find out if the monk knew any Wing Chun teachers. The monk recommended Wong Shun Leung. The name remained written on a piece of paper Nino carried around with him. And life continued as normal.

Until one day another musician mentioned a bone doctor who also taught Wing Chun. The two men decided to pay him a visit. When they arrived at Grenville Market they found a door with a brass plaque that had "Wong Shun Leung" written on it. Nino took out the paper from his pocket and realized that fate had brought him to the very same teacher that the monk had recommended. Nino remembers that first meeting well:

> *I can remember two people in the hall, with their arms interlocked and twisting. I asked them if their Sifu (teacher) was there. One of them shouted out "Sifu" and this small man in tracksuit bottoms and a sleeveless vest came out. He had a paunch belly and was smoking an unfiltered cigarette.*
>
> *We had a short chat. He asked me for my ID card and two photos and implied that he would check with a contact in the police whether or not I had a criminal record.*
>
> *At the time, I had no idea that this was the legendary "talking hands Wong," who had won so many challenge fights. All I knew was that an old monk on Lan Tao island had recommended him. As I began training, what really blew me away was the way that my sifu explained geometrical angles and tactics.*
>
> *Over the next few years, I trained with my sifu nearly every day and often up to seven hours a day. I also became friends with him and would sometimes go for a meal or a drink with him when we weren't training.*

> *Eventually, I was to become one of only a handful of students who completed the whole system with him. I can still remember the way that he carefully introduced each stage of the system in chronological order. As a teacher, I have tried to remember the system in the same order and present it to my students in the same way...*

By the early 1970s Bruce Lee's movies were becoming popular all over the world. His athleticism, charisma, and unique filmography were making Chinese Kung-fu a thing worthy of aspiration for many young people. Martial arts were becoming cool. For most people this would go no further than watching martial arts movies—Bruce Lee had almost single handedly reinvented the genre for a modern global audience—and acting out scenes in the playground. But for Loukas Kastrounis life would become much more serious.

> *I was born in Athens, Greece. Life was good. My father, George Kastrounis, was an accomplished violinist and had encouraged me to learn how to play classical piano. But when I was ten years old my father passed away and I was left to fend for myself with little family support. I had to cope with daily survival pretty much on my own, using my wits and thinking on my feet.*

Loukas's younger years were spent enjoying sports such as swimming and football (he was goalkeeper), and with much dedication he continued his musical and general education before he began studying hotel management and catering. Afterward he started working in hotels, bars, and discotheques in Greece. He was also developing an interest in the fighting arts.

> *Although I thoroughly enjoyed the films, I viewed the fighting scenes as untrue and simply as a good form of entertainment. However, Kung-fu schools were not common in Greece at the time and the closest thing on offer was Karate. The way I saw this Karate was that it had a greater focus on sport and belt-grading and this was not really what I was looking for.*
>
> *Through my interest in martial arts and boxing I discovered the beauty of fighting arts, but following visits to boxing clubs to see what they could offer, I decided not to join up. Why pay to have someone break your nose and teach you to get hit when you could go on the streets and get it done for free!*

Rather like Wong Shun Leung, Loukas's first instinct was to question the claims that people made. He knew intuitively that the romanticized version of fighting presented in movies was not an accurate reflection of the reality of conflict. Fighting was a brutal thing. And the protracted combat scenes that made for good cinematography were nothing like the fast, furious, and painful experience of real-life combat. To be an effective fighter one had to be fast, efficient, and economical. But not unlike Bruce Lee, Loukas had another side to his nature: a mischievous sense of humor and a penchant for practical jokes. In other words, the fighting system Loukas was looking for would have to be "stylish" as well as effective. Even to this day, Loukas reminds his students to move with grace and "look good" as they swiftly neutralize and end an incoming threat. The grunting and groaning of Karate, or the rolling about on the floor of Ju-jitsu would not suit him. Although he could not have known it at the time, Wing Chun was a natural fit for his personality.

> *I was still fascinated by boxing and martial arts and the way they could be used to look after oneself. I started training in a martial art called "Complete Wing Chun," but through reading books and analyzing what I was taught I felt something was missing.*

Analyzing what one is taught is the missing factor in most people's practice of anything. It is the reason people carry on following the unreasonable demands of those in authority without ever questioning what they are being told. When Loukas's father passed away, he had to question many assumptions. And he had learned, the hard way, that you cannot always believe what people tell you. Truth has a value that cannot be underestimated. In the end it is the truth that resolves conflicts, not lies and half-baked deceptions. The brutal honesty of Wing Chun is one of the reasons it is so effective. This honesty is reflected in the life and teachings of Wing Chun's greatest personalities—Dr. Leung Jan, Chan Wah Shun, Ng Jung So, Ip Man, Wong Shun Leung, and (somewhat paradoxically) in the legacy of Bruce Lee. Many of the wars that had touched the lives of these great masters had their origins in Europe. In the 1970s Greece too was untangling itself from the aftermath of some of the same wars.

> *On April 21, 1967, a group of right-wing colonels led by Colonel George Papadopoulos seized power in a coup d'état establishing the Regime of the Colonels. Civil liberties were suppressed, special military courts were established, and political parties were dissolved.*
>
> *Several thousand suspected communists and political opponents were imprisoned or exiled to remote Greek islands. Alleged US support for the junta is claimed to be the cause of rising anti-Americanism in Greece during and following the junta's harsh rule. The junta's early years also saw a marked upturn in the economy, with increased foreign investment and large-scale infrastructure works. The junta was widely condemned abroad, but inside the country, discontent began to increase only after 1970, when the economy slowed down.*
>
> *Even the armed forces, the regime's foundation, were not immune: in May 1973, a planned coup by the Hellenic Navy was narrowly suppressed, but led to the mutiny of the HNS Velos, whose officers sought political asylum in Italy. In response, junta leader Papadopoulos attempted to steer the regime toward a controlled democratization, abolishing the monarchy and declaring himself President of the Republic.*
>
> *On November 25, 1973, following the bloody suppression of Athens Polytechnic uprising on the 17th, the hardliner Brigadier Dimitrios Ioannides overthrew Papadopoulos and tried to continue the dictatorship despite the popular unrest the uprising had triggered. Ioannides's attempt in July 1974 to overthrow Archbishop Makarios, the Presi-*

dent of Cyprus, brought Greece to the brink of war with Turkey, which invaded Cyprus and occupied part of the island.

Senior Greek military officers then withdrew their support from the junta, which collapsed. Constantine Karamanlis returned from exile in France to establish a government of national unity until elections could be held. Karamanlis worked to defuse the risk of war with Turkey and also legalized the Communist Party, which had been illegal since 1947. His newly organized party, New Democracy (ND), won the elections held in November 1974 by a wide margin, and he became prime minister.

Following the 1974 referendum which resulted in the abolition of the monarchy, a new constitution was approved by parliament on June 19, 1975.[19]

And so at the age of nineteen Loukas was drafted into the Greek army serving from November 1976 to June 1979 as a personal driver and bodyguard to a Greek colonel. After leaving the army Loukas spent most of his time with his family—studying hospitality and management while working and training. In his late twenties he decided to come to England "just for fun," financing his venture with work as a bartender and, on occasions, door supervisor. Eventually he found a position in his field of study and decided to stay.

While working in the UK, Loukas continued his search for a good Wing Chun Kung-fu school and counts himself very lucky to have had the chance to attend a Nino Bernardo seminar being held at the time at the legendary Basement in London. Through this one seminar Loukas realized that he had found the truth behind Wing Chun that he had been searching for. Loukas then began as a private student of Nino's for the first two years and afterward he continued progressing in his Wing Chun and Kali studies at The Basement in London, under the supervision of Nino Bernardo and his senior students. Wong Shun Leung would frequently visit The Basement to work with the students. One of Bruce Lee's most respected students, Dan Inosanto, a living legend in his own right, would also visit the establishment. The atmosphere was informal and yet intensely focused. Loukas remembers those years well:

Sifu Nino Bernardo's famous Wing Chun Kung-fu school, "The Basement," opened its doors back in 1984. It was there that Nino Bernardo developed his reputation as one of Europe's most skillful and influential Wing Chun teachers. He was also Wong Shun Leung's senior UK representative until Sifu Wong's untimely death in 1997.

The school was located in the basement of a building close to a council estate on 60-64 Matthias Road, Stoke Newington, North London—not the most up-market area of London. In fact, it was quite the opposite.

---

19. Wikipedia, "History of Modern Greece," http://en.wikipedia.org/wiki/History_of_modern_Greece#Transition_to_democracy_.281973.E2.80.932009.29 140814.

The front gate of the building displayed a small, simple sign—"The Basement" logo. People went there only by word of mouth or if a person who already trained there had invited them. It was impossible to find the place unless you knew a student of the school or Nino himself had invited you.

Nino had no secret techniques and no secret school; he had a training school that he called his "play pen" and it had a very friendly atmosphere. Here, the Wing Chun training was hard, honest, and efficient, and there were no colorful belts or uniforms. Very soon the reputation of The Basement and Nino started to spread fast all over the world. During the 80s and 90s everyone within the martial arts world was speaking about The Basement school but only a few people knew its exact location.

Over the years The Basement has gained an almost mythical status. People have even questioned whether it ever really existed. It was a simple place but it had a magical feeling. It is impossible for me to describe this feeling; however, if I were to attempt a description, I would say it was like magic without magic.

As soon as you walked past the front door you would see students sweating, working hard and intensely but always with harmony among them and a respect for the system and each other. The training was so intense at times that injuries were inevitable. However, The Basement was the only place where if you did get hit, you would start laughing at your own mistake. Back then we all accepted that what we were studying was a martial art and as such it carried the inherent risk of injury but at the same time people didn't deliberately try to injure each other. From time to time, Nino would make everyone laugh and relax by telling one of his good old jokes, which most of the time had a deeper meaning behind them.

The Basement had four walls, no windows, and a small extractor fan. It did not have changing-rooms, chairs, or sofas to sit down on, nor was it air conditioned or heated. In the winter, you could see your breath as you did your forms, and during chi-sau training, the mirrors and walls would be dripping with condensation. The left wall had a drawing of a dragon, and in the middle of this dragon, the word "Basement" was written; however, you had to pay attention to be able to see it.

On the main wall of The Basement was a wooden dummy (muk yan chong), which had been given to Nino by Wong Shun Leung. It was made by one of the most well-known dummy-makers in Hong-Kong at the time. Above the dummy was a picture of Nino's teacher/sifu, the legendary Wong Shun Leung. (Wong was better known as "Gong Sau Wong," "king of talking with the hands.") Throughout the 50s and 60s he was undefeated in all of his challenges and was known as one of Ip Man's best students as well as the foremost instructor of Bruce Lee.

On each side of the wooden dummy were two calligraphic scrolls, given to Nino by Wong. These scrolls, which were written in Cantonese, stated that The Basement was *a kwoon (school) approved personally by Wong who had authorized Nino to teach Wing Chun in the UK.*

On the left-hand side of the wooden dummy I remember always seeing Nino's unicycle, which he would sometimes ride while simultaneously teaching.

Sometimes, he would pick up and play his guitar. He even invented a new game called "sucker ball," which was demonstrated on BBC TV and in the USA. Make no mistake, the training was always serious but Nino always had a colorful, eccentric, and unique style of teaching and delivery during The Basement years.

The Basement itself and all the senior students (si-hings) had class, style, and a love for the Wing Chun Kuen Kung-fu system. Nino and his Basement students also had a reputation as intelligent, skilled fighters.

Over the years, many students from around the world and from a wide array of professions, including actors, musicians, professors, managers, and doctors, came and trained at The Basement. In addition to this, seasoned martial artists, teachers, and students from various disciplines, including Wing Chun and Jeet Kune Do, as well as Special Forces from the UK and abroad also trained there.

Guru Dan Inosanto, Gass Magda, Larry Hartsell, and writer Bey Logan are just a few examples of the well-known martial artists who visited and trained at The Basement. Of course, Sifu Wong Shun Leung also gave regular seminars at The Basement. Nino, with his charismatic teaching and his clever ability to deliver the Wing Chun system, together with his students, placed The Basement at the center of attention within and outside the martial arts world—to many people it was "the mother" of Wing Chun schools.

The Basement no longer exists, having closed its doors in December 2000, but its legacy will live on forever. There will never be another place like "The Basement," but its name will shine for years to come and it will be remembered forever through each Wing Chun teacher and practitioner it has produced.

Nino has now moved to Ibiza, Spain, where he has set up Europe's first alternative Kung-fu school. His emphasis in recent years has been on the importance of learning Wing Chun for health and personal development. I consider myself very lucky to be one of Nino Bernardo's students and to have had the opportunity to train at The Basement. It was there that I learnt Wing Chun, about myself and in essence, was re-born. It was there where I made my best and true friends, who I am still in touch with, and train with to this day.

Before he left for Spain, Nino wrote Loukas a personal letter signed as a friend and as a teacher, thanking him for his time at The Basement and for what Loukas and his students have done for Wing Chun.

Nino taught me that by learning to control one's ego, anger, and pride in Wing Chun, the same attributes could be applied to improve one's everyday life.

Nino Bernardo and Wing Chun made me realize that you have to understand yourself; then you can understand and help your friends, family, children, and students to also discover the truth and not to force them but wait patiently. Wing Chun does not teach you knowledge, it teaches you to learn and discover one-self from your own feelings and emotions. Wing Chun makes you think faster, react faster. You need to practice it regularly. It is not just because you read, see, or are told something that you know it. Wing Chun also can help you in your everyday life. It is more than a system of fighting; it is also a way of thinking.

During his time at The Basement, Loukas met and trained with many *si-hing* (older Kung-fu brothers) and many *si-dai* (younger kung-fu brothers), including Segun Johnson, Guy Cofie, Dougy, Mark Wallach, Kenny Robinson, Kevin Lyn, John Turnbull, Steve Tabakin, Franco Regalzi, Wilfried Raimond, Jean Marc Noblot, Lemmy Man, Santi Pascual Martin, Jason Lai, Eddie Yuen, and many more.

As Loukas puts it, "Wing Chun is a complete system of self-defense, including boxing, trapping, kicking, grappling, and throwing. The only condition for attaining all this knowledge is time—first complete the entire system in order to understand it and understand yourself. Use the concepts and principles you have learned and then it will become your own way."

Loukas is a natural teacher who finds it easy to help each student understand the subtlety of Wing Chun in a way appropriate to his own background and temperament. He often does this through careful use of analogies and metaphors. He is often heard telling his beginner students that learning Wing Chun is like learning to write. First you follow the strokes as the teacher tells you. You learn the sounds of the letters. You learn the rules of punctuation and grammar. In the end you use those words, that grammar, and that punctuation to express yourself. And, ultimately, you develop your own handwriting.

In a fight it is not the one who hits first who wins but the one who hits last—and if you hit first and the opponent does not hit back . . . you've still hit last! Wing Chun teaches you how not to lose, and Kali familiarizes you with practical reactions to the threat posed by weapons.

Like Wong Shun Leung in Hong Kong, Loukas began to further his own training at home with seasoned martial artists joining him to learn from him. They trained in his garage from 1992 onward. It must have been an interesting spectacle for the neighbors—all these Karate, Taekwondo, Aikido, and other practitioners turning up to train. Perhaps Karate *kiais* and Taekwondo *kihaps* became regular sounds in the neighborhood. Interestingly, Wing Chun practitioners do most of their talking with their hands. There are no kiais in Wing Chun.

One day the martial artists had a sudden epiphany: there were just too many people turning up to fit in "The Garage"!

And so with Nino's authorization, Loukas opened the first Wing Chun school in Reading, Berkshire—The Reading Academy of Wing Chun and Kali. Since then the school's reputation has spread far and wide. Students who had started practicing Wing Chun in "The Garage" are still training today in the Reading Kwoon headquarters, helping newcomers along while continuing to refine their own practice.

Some of these practitioners have learnt the entire Wing Chun system from Sifu Loukas and are now certified instructors of The Reading Academy Of Wing Chun And Kali in their own right. Beginners, intermediate, and more advanced practitioners train together in quite a natural way. The atmosphere is relaxed but focused.

As one enters through the door towards Sifu Loukas's Reading kwoon, a narrow corridor turns sharply to the right. At the end of that corridor a precious art handed down from generation to generation, its roots in the fabulous past of ancient China, its branches extending out through the world, lives on. Interesting sounds carry through this corridor, inviting the visitor on. *Listen carefully! Here is a precious treasure preserved through the tempests of history, alive and well, growing and continuing, in the present and onto the future. There are no kiais here. Just the comforting sounds of fast footwork, pak-saus, shuffling feet, the clanking rhythm of the wooden dummies, and the intermittent sounds of laughter…*

PART TWO
THE SYSTEM

"With Kung-fu, the simpler, the better."
—*Grandmaster Dr. Leung Jan*[20]

Part Two attempts to provide a straightforward, comprehensive, and yet concise, guide to Wing Chun focusing on the most important aspects of training that benefit beginners and more experienced practitioners alike. The illustrations in this section are designed to help you better understand the text and to assist you with your own practice. Although there is no adequate substitute for a teacher, the text and illustrations are carefully crafted to assist you in your understanding and practice of Wing Chun regardless of your current level and experience. Like Wing Chun itself, we have tried to keep this section "economical" and "efficient" by keeping the explanations short and to the point while also pointing the way to deeper insights into Wing Chun.

---

20. Danny Connor and Chun Ip, *Wing Chun Martial Arts: Principles and Techniques* (Newburyport, MA: Weiser, 1992). 26.

5
WHAT'S THE BIG IDEA?
A Concise Overview of Wing Chun

In the previous section we suggested that if the best representatives of different martial artists were compelled to agree on the smallest number of essential principles, to come to a consensus—not about technique—but about the "concepts" that are the most important in a fight, if they were being honest and frank, they would come up with a list that describes the foundations of Wing Chun. These foundations may be expressed in different

Figure 5-1. Sifu Loukas carefully scrutinizes Nick's "fook-sau." The keen eye of the master looks out for many fine details in his student: the use of two hands—one pulling back, one going forward; the center of gravity of the body; the central line theory—crossing the elbow through the centerline. The body should be in perfect stillness.

ways but the underlying meaning is the same. These essential principles are explained here. Taken as a whole and reflected on deeply they represent the entire system of Wing Chun. And they answer a reasonable question: "What is Wing Chun Kung-fu?"

- In its essence it is the most simple, direct, and efficient Kung-fu system. If a response to an attack is not simple, direct, and efficient it is not (good) Wing Chun.
- Wing Chun is a complete fighting system relying on counterattacks. *Complete* means it does not need recourse to principles or "techniques" outside of itself. *Counterattack* does not necessarily mean you do not hit "first" but does mean that you hit last (see previous section). The Wing Chun practitioner uses both arms, both hands, both legs, and both feet. He uses elbows knees, wrists, palms, fists, and all the other "weapons" at his disposal according to the principles.
- At its most simple Wing Chun uses economy of motion, flow from one move to the next, leverage, and straight-line strikes. There are no long circular motions in Wing Chun as the shortest distant between two points is a straight line. The Wing Chun fighter takes the lines given by the opponent; he does not need to force his way through.
- It uses body mechanics, structure, and posture to neutralize a threat. To be effective the practitioner of Wing Chun learns to react naturally to an attack with forward energy. His body structure and mechanics enable to him sense the correct lines of entry, to eliminate an incoming threat, and to act spontaneously without "calculating" or "pondering" the next move.
- The less effort and force used, the better your Wing Chun. There is no need to engage in grappling or fancy blocks when you respond naturally to your opponent. Even if your opponent attempts to grapple with you the principles of body mechanics and straight-line energies hold true. Grappling and wrestling waste too much energy. The structure and principles of Wing Chun hold true in any type of conflict.
- The Wing Chun practitioner feels the strength of the opponent's attack and intuitively senses the weakness. He responds immediately without hesitation to intercept and strike.
- When the Wing Chun fighter is reacting to an opponent's actions he should cultivate the same frame of mind that he would have when reacting to natural danger. But in this case the reactions are the most mechanically efficient and intelligent, driven by forward energies. In other words, this is a refining of the natural flinch response we all possess.
- The Wing Chun practitioner intercepts the incoming attack and follows the outgoing retreat. But to trap and hit, or to strike the opponent before he strikes you, is the best solution.

These concepts are actually very simple and most honest people with experience in combat would agree with them. Loukas likes to tell beginners that the first thing we do is "tidy up" the mess. This is the case especially if the beginner to Wing Chun has been practicing another martial art and has picked up unrealistic and overly complicated habits. It is often worse if they are "masters" of an art, unless they have had real fighting experience in which case they intuitively understand the principles. Perhaps this is what Bruce Lee meant by "daily decrease, not daily increase." All these principles are trained and refined in the first Wing Chun Form. The "big idea" of Wing Chun is therefore not really a big idea at all. No wonder the first and most important training form of Wing Chun is called Siu Nim Tau—"The Little Idea Form."

6
SIU NIM TAU
The First Form, the Last Form

"When the highest type of men hear the Way, with diligence they're able to practice it;
When average men hear the Way, some things they retain and others they lose;
When the lowest type of men hear the Way, they laugh out loud at it.
If they didn't laugh at it, it couldn't be regarded as the Way."

—*Lao Tzu, Te-Tao Ching* [21]

Siu Nim Tau ("The Little Idea Form") is the first of three "empty hand" forms the Wing Chun practitioner learns. Actually "learn" is not quite the right word here. As long as a person practices Wing Chun they will *study* the first form over and over again, and they will practice it every day.

The three "empty-hand" or non-weapon forms are:
1. *Siu Nim Tau:* "Little Idea Form"
2. *Chum Kiu:* "Seeking the Bridge"
3. *Biu Jee:* "Thrusting Fingers"

After the student has learned these forms they are then introduced to the Wooden Dummy movements and the two weapon forms—the Long Pole and the Butterfly Knives.

All of these forms are embedded or encoded within the first form. In other words Siu Nim Tau contains within it the concepts and principles of the entire system. For this reason alone it needs to be performed slowly and thoughtfully. As one's Wing Chun improves, so does one's understanding of Siu Nim Tau, and as one's understanding of Siu Nim Tau improves, so does one's Wing Chun. It is therefore the beginning and the end form of Wing Chun.

---

21. Robert G. Henricks, (trans), *Lao-Tzu Te-Tao Ching: A New Translation Based on the Recently Discovered Ma-Wang Tui Texts* (New York, NY: Ballantine Books, 1992), 9.

The first form teaches us how to delete the myriad thoughts that are going through our brain, to quiet the mind. Not to *think*, but to *feel*. When done correctly it teaches us patience. Loukas recalls that his own teacher used to say that in a fight we must never rush in, never fight angry, and only hit when the opportunity arises. This is just one of the many "attitudes" that Siu Nim Tau teaches.

Many Qigong (Chi Kung) practitioners who have come to study Wing Chun have been amazed by the advanced Qigong and energy work contained in Siu Nim Tau—particularly the first part of the form. Like some of the most advanced Qigong forms found in the so-called "internal" or "soft" arts, its movements are outwardly quite simple, but performed slowly with attention to energy and body alignment, they enable the practitioner to develop an extraordinary understanding of *rootedness* necessary for advanced energy work. Typical of advanced practice, the skill in performing Siu Nim Tau lies in paying attention to the details and letting the form reveal to you an understanding of your own body structure and alignment.

Among the many things that this form prepares the student for is touching hands and testing one's Wing Chun with a partner. It does this by developing the ability of the student to move his body without thinking; to refine and improve his structure; to "bypass" the mental block that often hinders or delays an appropriate response and free the practitioner to move swiftly without hesitation.

At The Basement school, students who could not do a long first form were not allowed to touch hands with other practitioners. A novice can be recognized by how quickly they perform the Siu Nim Tau. Sifu Loukas's beginning students are advised to increase the time spent in the form gradually. Beginners should not perform Siu Nim Tau in less than fifteen minutes. Advanced practitioners should be performing the form for thirty minutes to an hour every day.

Another mistake that beginners make is rushing to memorize the hand shapes and arm movements without paying attention to the details. In order to perform Siu Nim Tau correctly you should pay attention to:

1. The movement of the hands (these should move in a constant flow without stopping. As much as possible, you should follow the path that aligns correctly to your centerline and body structure.
2. The position of the hips
3. The position of the shoulders
4. The position of the spine
5. The elbows
6. The horse stance

This may sound like a tall order but by paying attention to the following points you can begin to develop a good understanding of Siu Nim Tau.

Make sure the upper body does not slouch. Stand as if there is a string or line of energy extending out from your spine and upper body pulling your head upward. This is sometimes called *rising yang energy*. Keep your knees bent and your feet pigeon-toed in the horse stance. Rotate your pelvis thrusting your hips forward and upward and squeeze your thighs together as if holding a ball between them and rooting downwards from your lower body. This is sometimes called *sinking yin energy*.

When you begin to practice Siu Nim Tau in this way, energy is generated from the heels up through the lower body to the hips, from the hips along an imaginary line connecting to your elbows, and through your arms into your hands, making the hands feel like a whip. This is called *lat sau chi chung*—"forward hand energy."

With diligent practice, the lat sau chi chung becomes more pronounced, and the practitioner is able to feel the hands moving like a whip, driven with energy generated from the lower body and through the hips into the elbows. "Only when the first form is practiced in this manner," says Sifu Loukas, "is the whole body engaged in the form. And only then do we have mind and body connected, working together."

Wong Shun Leung would remind Sifu Loukas that when someone is thinking before executing a "technique" they are not doing Wing Chun. This needs to be remembered at all times—during the forms, when doing drills, when practicing chi-sau with a partner. This idea of "not-thinking" starts to become a reality when you can relax and be at ease with Siu Nim Tau while at the same time performing it as accurately as possible.

Sim Nim Tau: The Form Step by Step

6: SIU NIM TAU

6: SIU NIM TAU 57

6: SIU NIM TAU

6: SIU NIM TAU

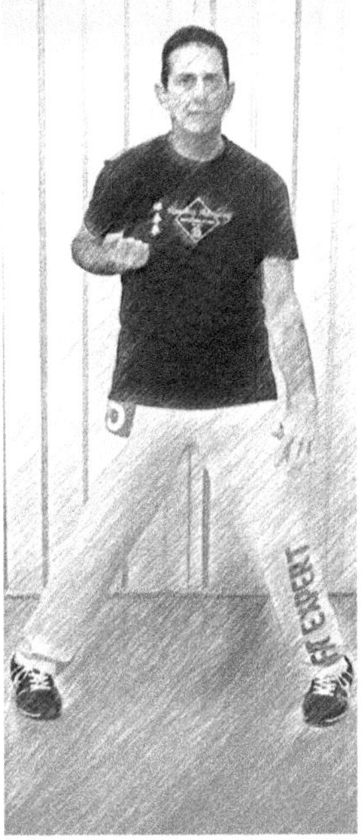
FIT EXPERT
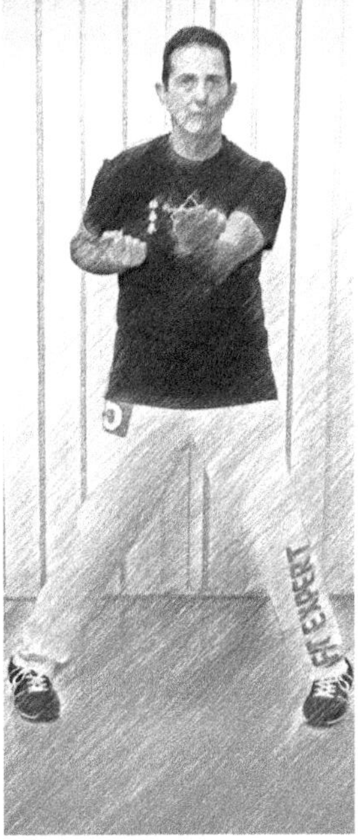
FIT EXPERT
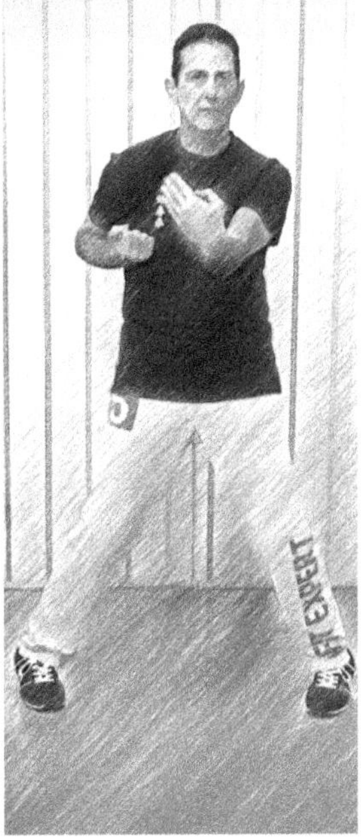
FIT EXPERT
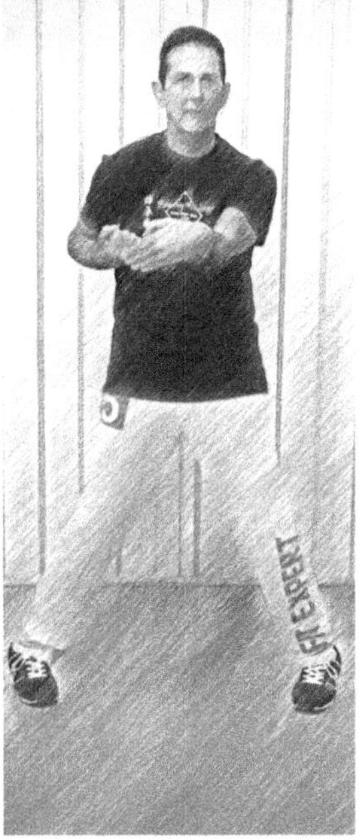
FIT EXPERT
FIT EXPERT
FIT EXPERT
FIT EXPERT
FIT EXPERT

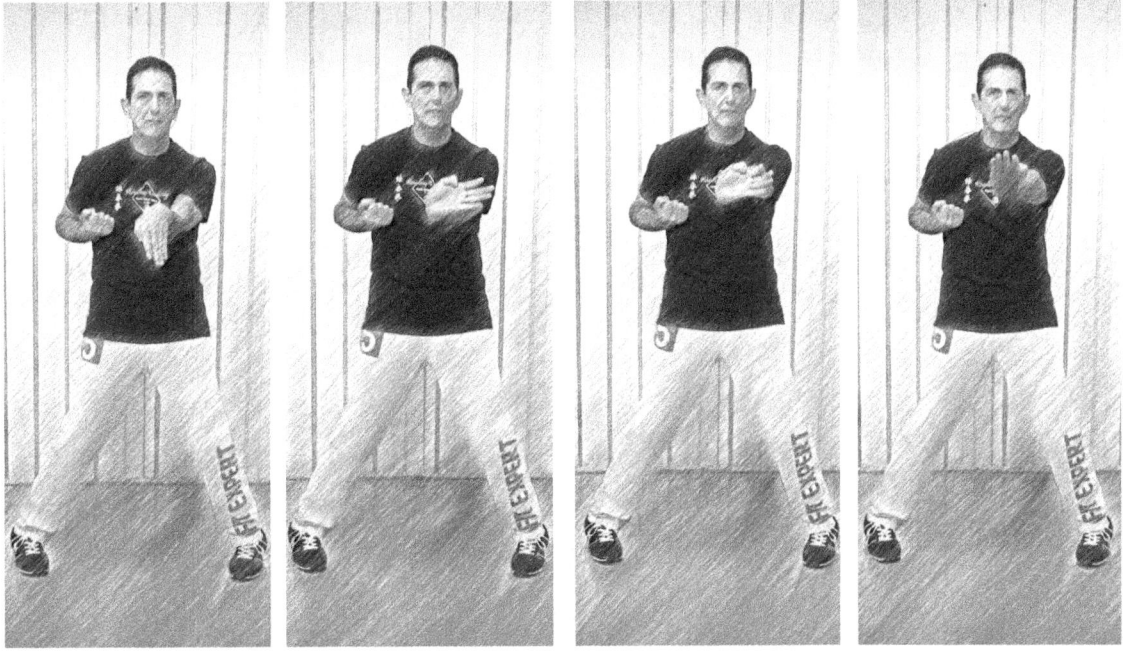

72 WING CHUN IN-DEPTH

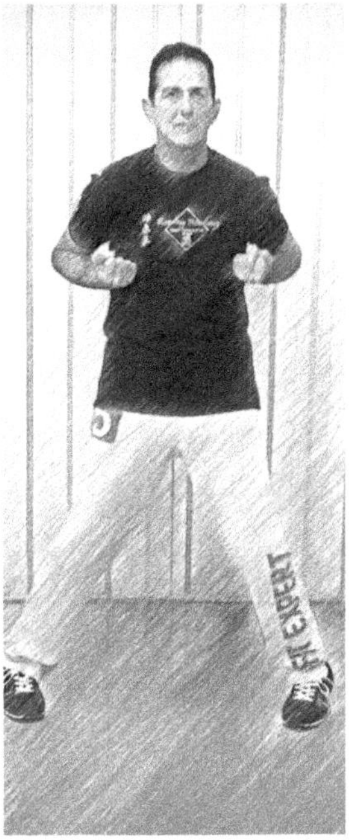
FIT EXPERT

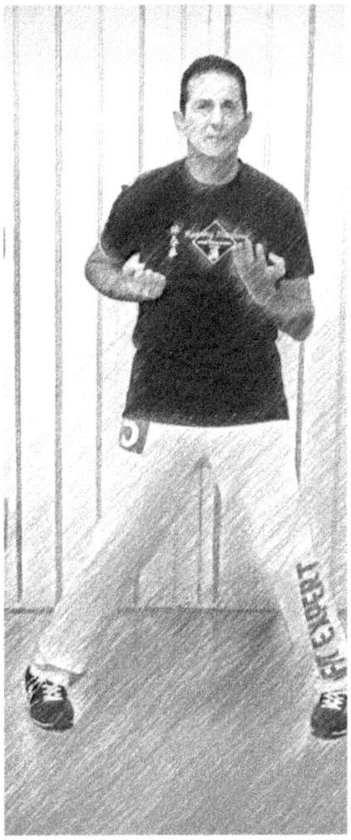
FIT EXPERT

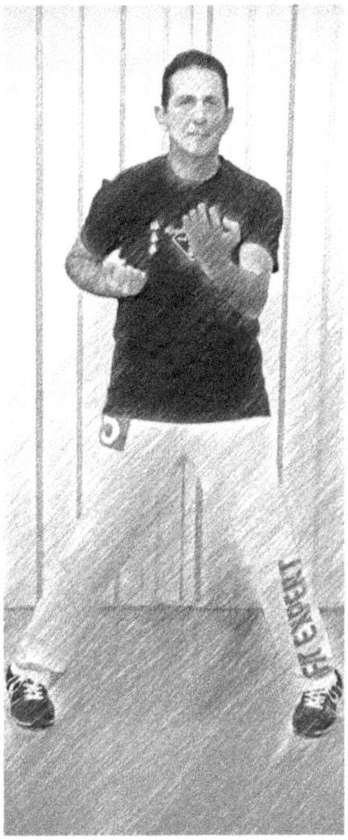
FIT EXPERT

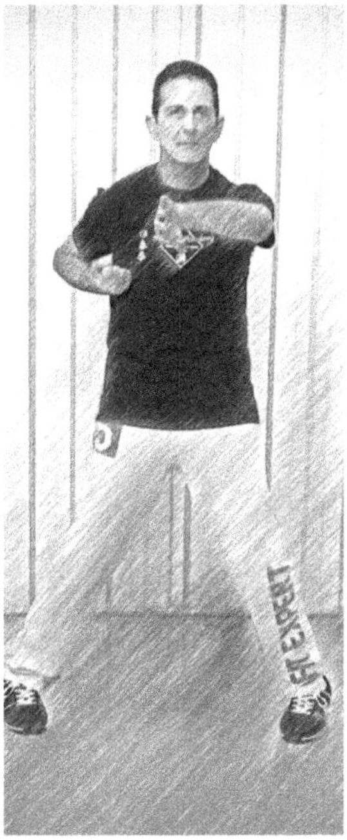
FIT EXPERT

FIT EXPERT

FIT EXPERT

FIT EXPERT

FIT EXPERT

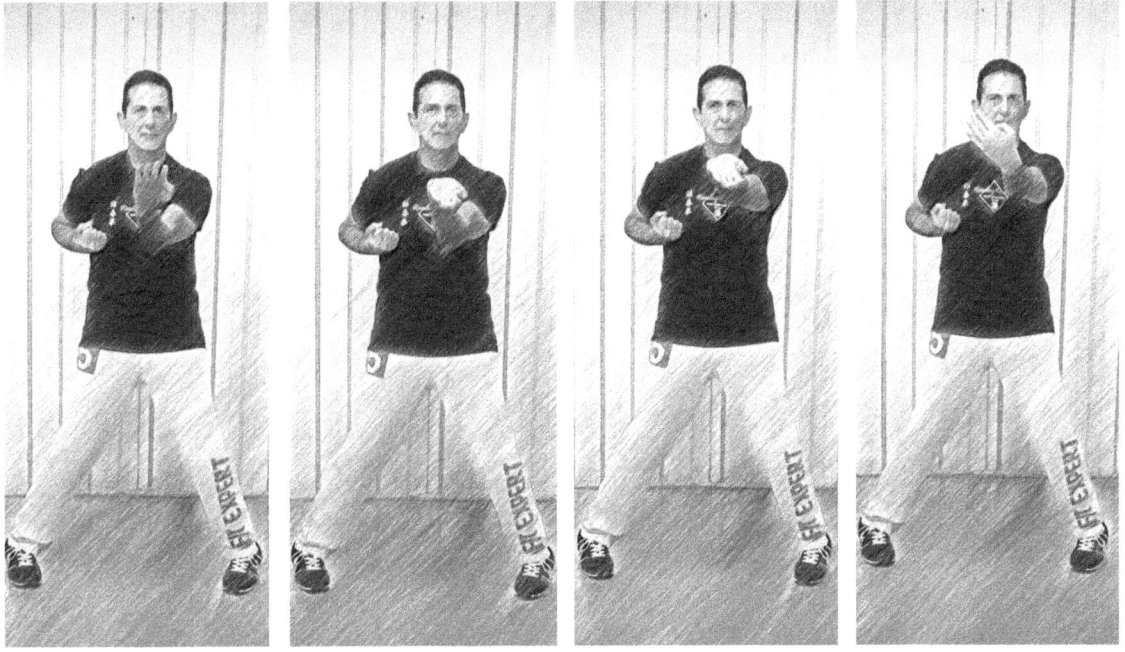

6: SIU NIM TAU

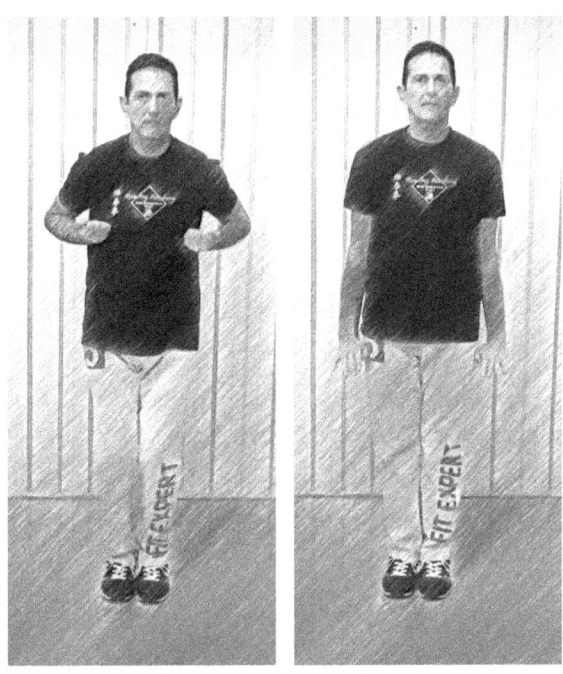

BASIC HAND SHAPES

Now that we have clarified the important details of Siu Nim Tau we can look at the basic hand shapes that are found in the form. As mentioned earlier, beginners often make the mistake of rushing to learn the hand shapes first rather than thinking about the energies, lines, and structures mentioned above. In a sense, the hand shapes are secondary to those more important considerations. There are three basic hand shapes in the first form:

1. *Tan-Sau* (remember Tan-sau Ng?)
2. *Fook-Sau*
3. *Bong-Sau*

When making the hand shapes it is worthwhile remembering that the structure is stronger when the hand shapes form three angles rather than two.

Tan-sau Visual Cues

Figure 6-1. Sifu Loukas tests Nick's tan-sau. "We're testing the energy of the elbow and the forearm to see if the elbow is connected into the hip and into the leg. This is called lat sau chin chung (forward spring loaded energy)." As he checks and adjusts his student's hands Loukas mentions the etymology of the term tan-sau: "Tan means 'to lay'; sau means 'hands.' So we have tan-sau: 'lay the hands.'"

Figure 6-2. "Here we're looking for the energy to go from the elbows into the fingers; and the forearm to go forward through Nick's centerline."

Figure 6-3. Tan-sau moving forward (front view). Here you can see the use of two hands with a perfect body structure. Notice the horse stance; the hand pulling back is activated; the energy is going from the ground through the legs into the hips and forward through the forearm into the centerline. Through this exercise we are discovering and testing our own body mechanics.

Fook-sau Visual Cues

Figure 6-4. Fook-sau: even in the illustration we can see that the wrist is bent inwards. We do not strike with the fook-sau as that would damage the hands. Fook is a 'hook." Sau is the "hand." The more the wrist is bent, the more you connect and tense the forearm through the elbows. Sensitivity develops from there. Fook-sau is "receiving hands," not "attacking hands" so you need to be able to feel through the inner forearm from the wrists to the elbow.

Figure 6-5. "Here again we are testing the elbow to make sure it is supporting the fook-sau." Sifu Loukas pushes Nick's hands from the wrist deliberately while touching his elbow to see if the energy from his push is going through Nick's elbows down into his hips, legs, and into the ground. If the structure is correct Nick's body naturally moves as one unit backward in response to Sifu's pushing hand. (See tan chi-sau and choi-ma/soi-ma referred to in Part Three below.)

Figure 6-6. The fingers should be pointing towards the navel—this creates the correct tension on the inner forearm which helps transmit the energy appropriately. However note that this is how it is done in the form in order to develop body mechanics. Do not make the mistake of some practitioners who misunderstand this and maintain too much tension or stiffness in their forearms in a real fight, which limits their flexibility.

Figure 6-7. Sifu Loukas applies pressure on Nick's wrist (not the back of his hand) in order to check the alignment and structure of the fook-sau. If the alignment is correct his forearm will not collapse. Instead it will move just a little back, activating his hips and sending the energy downwards through his legs.

Figure 6-8. Side view of correct fook-sau. Also notice the Wing Chun horse stance and alignment of the lower body.

Bong-sau Visual Cues

Figure 6-9. Bong-sau is "receiving hands." The energy is going from the shoulder to the elbow and not to the forearm. The actual bong-sau is from the shoulder to the elbow. The forearm from the elbow to the hands is the "bridge"—sometimes referred to as the "arm bridge."

As a receiving hand the purpose of the bong-sau is to redirect a forceful attack by using the hips by shifting. In the form this is represented as a stationary position, but in reality the hips will shift (body pivots on its central axis) in order to redirect the attack away from the centerline. It can also be used as a throwing technique (see Chapter 10, below). Bong-sau is not a strong defensive hand; rather, it is a weak hand and should not be used frequently. Often we see practitioners using bong-sau in double hands but it does not mean it should be used all the time in a fight. In all his real-life fights Sifu Loukas only recalls having to use the bong-sau once in response to a surprise forward attack where the assailant came in with great force. Loukas's bong-sau came out instinctively sending the assailant flying off into the wall as a result of his own force. The fight was over immediately.

Figure 6-10. Sifu examines the triangle shape formed from Nick's shoulder to his elbow, to his wrist (three angles). The wrist must not be lifted higher than the elbow, and the elbow must not be lifted higher than the shoulder. The rotation should be originating from the wrist, not from the elbow. If the elbow lifts it can cause damage to the shoulder, and also slows down the movement resulting in a "lifting" of the opponent.

Figure 6-11. Sifu Loukas checks Nick's fingers to make sure that they are relaxed. This reduces tension in the hands and helps make the fingers, hands, and arm act as one unit. Also the fingers are "tucked-in" so as to not prevent risk of injury.

Figure 6-12. Side view during practice of the Siu Nim Tau form showing the horse stance and correct bong-sau position.

You cannot lift a heavy opponent with the bong-sau. It is a throwing movement not a lifting one. The redirection of force travels downwards allowing this to become a throwing technique or opening up other options for the counterattack.

Figure 6-13. Sifu Loukas points out how Nick's elbow is aligned with his hip. You can also see clearly that the elbow is not raised higher than the shoulders.

Figure 6-14. Front view of the bong-sau showing correct alignment of the entire body.

The Use of Two Hands

It is also worth noting that in the second section of the form two hands are used together. One should bear in mind that this does not mean that you will need to use two hands in this way when executing a technique in a live combat situation. In any case both hands are always active during Siu Nim Tau in all of the sections.

*

PUNCHING

The punch should always be executed from the centerline with the small knuckle aiming towards the opponent's nose or face. The elbows should drive the hand, not the shoulders, and the punch should "swing" from the hip. These points are very important.

When your hands are open or outside the centerline and the opponent launches a punch to your centerline, you should intercept by punching to the point where your fist would end up if it were a centerline punch, but *without* bringing your hand to your centerline first. To do otherwise would be a waste of time. This should be considered carefully.

As you continue to improve your Siu Nim Tau you must also practice the straight punches outside of the form. "It is a must to practice the straight punches daily," says Sifu Loukas. He insists that students should average around 2,000 punches a day in order to develop the coordination of both hands, accuracy, speed, and flow. Most importantly, this practice trains the hands to strike automatically whenever an opening becomes available.

The next step is to start practicing hitting the wall bag. This helps strengthen the knuckles and gets the hands used to hitting objects. Without practicing hitting the wall bag your Wing Chun punch will not be good in combat.

Also you must pay attention to differences between hitting a wall bag and punching in the air. When practicing punching in the air, the punches should be fast, using both hands simultaneously. One hand should pull back just a little while the other one is punching as straight as possible. However, when hitting the wall bag the punches are vertical and they should not be practiced fast. The first exercise is to improve speed. The second is to train for power and toughen up the knuckles.

Figure 6-15

Punch Principles Visual Guide

Figure 6-16

"What we call, in Wing Chun terms, the chain straight punches."
The energy comes from the elbows through the forearms exploding into the fist. It is very important that your fist must be in a straight line with your arm, otherwise you can damage the wrist. It is like a piston with the energy going from the elbow into the hands. When striking, do so with the knuckles—with the first point of impact being the small knuckle of the pinky finger followed by the other two large knuckles.
To ensure the target is on the centerline take an imaginary straight line from the nose to the knuckles of the fist to avoid the effect of parallax shift.

Figure 6-17

Figure 6-18

"What we see here in these illustrations is the optical illusion of Wing Chun."
You see the leading hand, but actually in Wing Chun we are hitting with the rear hand—which is already charged and loaded. The first hand, which has been extended, is pulling back; the rear hand is actually striking. Think of pulling back with the lead hand while simultaneously pushing out with the rear hand. The concept is to land multiple strikes against the same target. The idea should be of a small gun firing rapidly rather than a large gun firing a massive shot with delay in between each shot. Strikes should be rapid, simultaneous, continuous, and directed to a small target.

Figure 6-19

Figure 6-20

Imagine a small target like a small circle with the punches landing in the center of that circle without pause. Then imagine a small dot in the middle of a small circle just big enough for your fist to fit through. (For example, the invisible compass point from which a circle is drawn.)

Why do we hit with the small knuckle instead of the big knuckles? The reason is that the small knuckle is like a knife point penetrating internally into the target with the remaining large knuckles

Figure 6-21

Figure 6-22

following. The Wing Chun strike is therefore an internal strike, not just an external strike. Imagine an iron ball striking and hitting the surface with the impact extending into the inside of the body.

In the type of punching depicted in Figures 6-17 to 6-22, knocking out the opponent from the leading hand is unlikely, just as in boxing it is highly unlikely that an opponent can be knocked out from the jab.

The Wing Chun rear hand can be seen as the cross but without using the shoulder. Instead the shoulder needs to be tucked in to allow the whole body to follow the hands as one unit. So don't think of knocking out the opponent with the lead hand—if you do manage this think of yourself as lucky! It's the use of the whole body to transmit force into the small point of the striking surface (the small knuckle) and the target surface (the small circle area of the opponent). Think of force=mass times acceleration (f=ma). Which is why Wong Shun Leung used to call Wing Chun a scientific fighting system making use of body mechanics.

Think of punching at the speed of light. However, to practice this you must begin by practicing with stillness. This has to be done deliberately in order to learn how to go through the centerline. Eventually you'll practice together with the footwork.

Another important point here is that the elbows, as they return back, must "sink" in order to be loaded for the next punch. They must sink just enough to be locked but not sink all the way back. When you pull back it's like you pull something to you. This pulling force drives the opposite pushing force of the striking (rear) hand. In other words you pull the lead hand by sinking the elbow toward your hip to generate the opposite energy of the rear hand striking out. Think of an old-fashioned gun—it needs to reload with the lead hand coming back in order for the rear hand to strike out.

When you're punching, think about your elbows sinking while watching your wrists and keeping your eyes on the target to ensure that your fist goes through the target out of the other side. Think of "multiple simultaneous activities."

Finally, it is worth pointing out that in many styles of martial arts, practice is based on circular motion. Wing Chun practice, however, is based on a "forward circular exchange." Receive and attack; be the last to strike. Or as Sifu Loukas often says: "Be late to be on time." You must research this well.

(Note the subtlety of changes in each of the above illustrations as the punch is executed. None of the images are being repeated although it may seem like that to the untrained eye.)

*

HORSE STANCE AND "FIGHTING STANCE"

It is important to mention here something about the "horse stance" (*yee jee kim yeung ma*). Some people are put off by Wing Chun when they see the Siu Nim Tau being practiced, especially when they notice the "pigeon-toed" low horse stance, with knees bent and thighs pressing inwards, and the practitioner facing "square on" as it were. They assume that this is how Wing Chun practitioners fight. Sifu Loukas always reminds his beginner students that they should not allow themselves to be deluded. The fixed and square-on facing stance is not how we would face an opponent in a real fight.

One of the reasons for this misconception is that in many other martial arts the forms, or *katas* or patterns are actually taught as "fighting" forms. This limits those arts to set-piece encounters—"your opponent throws a jab, you do this…" Wing Chun's approach is quite different. Siu Nim Tau, as we have mentioned, helps develop feelings, energies, lat sau chi chung (forward hand energy or what Loukas calls "forward spring-loaded energy"), structure, and so forth. These are the attributes, concepts, and motor-memory skills necessary to fight well according to Wing Chun's principles (outlined at the beginning of this chapter). Actually, Wing Chun practitioners tend to fight from a "natural stance," sometimes called a "shuffle stance" or *chor ma*. This comes about when you pivot from the horse-stance to the right or left. So long as the practitioner is careful to retain the structure and energies developed when doing Siu Nim Tau in the horse-stance, the center of gravity will remain along his centerline even in the natural stance and the "feeling" of balance, energy, and stability trained in Siu Nim Tau will remain with him. This is the point. The yee jim kim yeung ma maintained in Siu Nim Tau enables us to understand how to maintain the optimum structure and lines when we are in chor ma, to relocate our structure after having launched a kick or other attack, or even after having lost our balance momentarily. In other words the feeling we have in the horse stance should be the same in the natural stance. This is the stance that the Wing Chun practitioner fights from.

When the ignorant, casual observer sees Siu Nim Tau being practiced so diligently by both beginners and advanced practitioners it is only right that he fails to understand what is happening. If he laughs out loud remarking that if anyone fights like that they will be in trouble, then all the better. What such people have failed to see or understand is the incredibly efficient genius of Wing Chun. It is only proper that they should remain blissfully ignorant.

Fighting Stance Visual Cues

Figure 6-23. "How would you like to be hit?" Sifu Loukas in a typical Wing Chun fighting stance. The body is free to pivot in any direction the attack is coming from. At no point should your centerline be directly facing the opponent. This is the Wing Chun fighting stance. Loukas's hands are central but his body's centerline is turned away from the opponent. It's a misunderstanding to face your opponent with the typical Wing Chun horse stance found in Su Nim Tau because it will expose you to hits. Nick is ready to attack Sifu here. So Loukas keeps his centerline away from Nick's direction of attack while also being able to pivot his body in response to Nick's angle of attack. In a sense Sifu is asking a question to Nick: "How would you like to be hit? Let me know so that I can oblige."

7

CHI-SAU

The Heart and Soul of Wing Chun

CHI-SAU DRILLS

As your practice and understanding of Siu Nim Tau improves the teacher will gradually prepare you for chi-sau training. This is done by performing certain basic drills until you can do them naturally in a relaxed state. The three basic drills are:

1. *Tan Chi-Sau* (Single Sticky Hands)
2. *Luc-Sau* (Double Hands)
3. *Fan-Sau* (Alternating Hands)

A simple way to encourage forward energy when doing these drills, and when doing *chi sau* in general, is to imagine you have no hands and that your forearms (i.e., from your wrist to your elbows) are wooden stumps. None of these drills should be taught or practiced in a hurry. The key to success here is continuous repetition.

*

MOVING THE STANCE FORWARD AND BACKWARD

Choi-mo (forward) and choi-ma (backward) are drills that help a student learn how to move backward and forward while maintaining the correct structure. As your practice of Wing Chun improves you will come to realize that the footwork of the art is also embodied within the static practice of Siu Nim Tau. But there is a danger that you can become too habituated to standing still when fighting or practicing chi-sau. For this reason, Sifu Loukas will watch his students closely and may introduce exercises to ensure that you do not develop bad habits that have to be untaught later on.

*

MORE ADVANCED TWO-PERSON DRILLS

Further drills to enhance the practitioner's understanding of Wing Chun include "combination" drills performed in pairs. Among these are *lap-sau/pac sau/tan-sau* combinations; *bong-sau/lap-sau/gan-sau* combinations; and Five-Elements Drills designed to improve coordination and trapping. All of these drills help the student understand *chi-sau* and ready him or her for light chi-sau practice.

The drills can and should be done without a partner as well ("shadow boxing") in order to improve speed and encourage the use of the lower body.

*

ON THE PRACTICE OF CHI-SAU

Chi-sau is Cantonese for "sticky hands" and is one of the most important exercises in the Wing Chun system. Without chi-sau, forms and drills are useless. Forms and drills are the body of Wing Chun while chi-sau is the heart of the system. But Chi-sau does not only prepare you for the fight. It also teaches you how to deal with stress, teaching you how to respond by panicking in a constructive way, to react without thinking, and yet still be accurate and quick. It combines hands and legs, and increases the ability for multiple, simultaneous activities as well as improving fitness, health, coordination, balance and developing the counterattack reaction—the "automatic pilot."

By practicing chi-sau, you learn how to use your body effectively. When you have been hit, you know you have made a mistake. Primarily, the objective is not to look for the hit, but to ensure that you do not get hit. This is practiced in chi-sau by teaching your body to move fast, get out of the danger and then counterattack effectively, without thought being involved. By doing this, chi-sau is the perfect preparation for the fight. However, chi-sau is not only aimed at fighting. It also teaches you how to deal with all kinds of stress. Chi-sau helps you to understand how to use your body naturally, effectively, and bring out your intelligence.

You have to remember that no one can teach you how to fight—every fight is different. When soldiers train, they don't kill each other but try to condition the body and mind up to the highest level so that if they need to go to war, they are prepared.

When training in Wing Chun the key is to train hard, regularly, and with the right school and you will be ready to use Wing Chun if necessary. Wing Chun will definitely bring out the best in you, in your relationships, your job, so that whatever you do, you will do it better. Chi-sau is the essence of Wing Chun. It is the primary tool for the training of instantaneous response for which Wing Chun is so famous. It is through chi-sau training that the practitioner develops his sense of touch, to feel the flow of energy of the opponent, so he can absorb and neutralize the attack and counter.

In chi-sau one must be like water, seeking the course of least resistance, avoiding the strong and attacking the weak. Chi-sau integrates this sense of touch with the fighting techniques that the Wing Chun practitioner has mastered in the first two hand forms and the Wooden Dummy, so that all flow together and are applied without thinking, without waiting for the mind to make a decision on which defense or attack technique to apply. Feel the flow of the energy of the opponent and react, be like water, seeking the least resistance, be direct, "panic," move, and Do Not Think!

In this way, through chi-sau the Wing Chun motto becomes real: *receive what comes, follow what goes, and attack when there is emptiness or when the hand disengages.*

Chi-Sau Visual Cues

Figure 7-1

Figure 7-2

Figure 7-3

Figure 7-4

Chi-sau practice up close. "Here we are emphasizing a lot on trapping hands."
Observe closely how Sifu Loukas and Nick engage in chi-sau practice. Sifu has immobilized Nick's hand while simultaneously offering a threat and pulling Nick downwards into a lap-sau cycle in order to strike with the rear hand (see above on straight punches). Again the push and pull can be clearly seen at work here. Wong Shun Leung used to say, "Without pull and push there is no Wing Chun."

Figure 7-5

Figure 7-6

Figure 7-7

Figure 7-8

Chi-sau teaches us trapping hands—one hand is trapping two; the other hand is striking. In the first and second forms as well as in the Wooden Dummy techniques the focus is on trapping hands and disturbing the opponent's structure as can be seen in these illustrations.

Figure 7-9

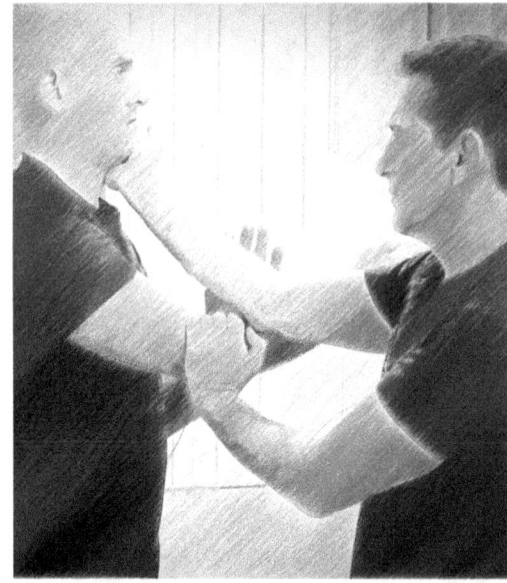

Figure 7-10

In Figures 7-9 and 7-10 you can see Sifu is striking the nearest target with his elbow (which can lead into an armlock technique). At the same time he is provoking Nick to attack so as to be able to respond with a counterattack. Or we could say he is asking Nick a question-setting him up for an intercept and counter–strike.

In Figure 7-11 Nick has taken the bait, leading Sifu to execute a pak-sau trapping Nick's hand and simultaneously striking from the opposite hand.

Figure 7-11

SIFU LOUKAS'S PERSONAL REFLECTIONS ON CHI-SAU

"When I started training with Sifu Nino Bernado—one of the few people who had completed the entire system directly from Sifu Wong Shun Leung—I knew nothing of Wong's reputation. I didn't know that he was a famous street fighter. I didn't know that he had been Bruce Lee's main Kung-fu instructor. I'm pleased I didn't know this then, because my ignorance allowed me to listen to my sifu without any preconceived ideas.

"Obviously most of what my sifu taught was about fighting. Nino and Wong were certainly not pacifist monks and they did not meditate. Instead they would talk about using fear, anger, and frustration to win fights by channeling these emotions in a positive way. Nino and Wong were very domineering and direct in their chi-sau. But they would also use it as a tool to read the character of others, to develop entries and to train themselves to cope with the intense stress that comes about in fighting. Many people nowadays have only heard about this side of Nino and Wong. But many of my students have witnessed Nino's teaching first hand.

"Training regularly with my sifu for over twenty-two years (including private training for at least two years) allowed me to pick up certain undercurrents. For example, although Nino wouldn't try and develop the personalities and characters of his students, he took great pleasure in observing how they developed and changed through their training in Wing Chun. During my time in his kwoon, my own friends noticed my personality changing for the better. I have since learned to regard this as one of the positive side effects of learning Wing Chun.

"When I opened the Reading Academy in 1992 one of the most difficult things that I found was the way that 'Western' students would ask for in-depth explanations of what they were meant to be doing, rather than just doing it. In Hong Kong, asking questions like that would be deemed disrespectful. However, in those days I was a new instructor and had to adapt to my students. I began searching for ways to describe Wing Chun so that my students would understand.

"It was during this period of intense study that I began to think of chi-sau as a fight-like game that helps practitioners develop certain 'side-effects.' Chi-sau uses both hemispheres of the brain, helping us develop awareness of our bodies, improving our skills in other areas and developing a sort of 'ruthless' intelligence. Another side effect involves trying to read the intent or character of another practitioner through physical contact with them. As I went further along this road I began to think of the system as a whole, as a clever self-development tool that can be used by fighters and others to develop and sharpen certain attributes." (Perhaps it was used in this way by the non-fighting Opera Performers to improve their stage work and performances.)

"We can use a screwdriver to stir our coffee just as easily as we can use it to remove a screw. We don't need to change the design of a tool to find a new use for it. This led to a deeper understanding of chi-sau—as we began to focus on underlying structures, body-mechanics, tactics, strategies.

"In my teaching I do promote the fighting aspects of the system. There have been times in my life when I have chosen to fight. I'm not proud of that. But because of my work (as general manager in night-clubs) in the past some fights were inevitable. In fact, were necessary. However there is no doubt that violence is unintelligent negative behavior. Quite frankly it is inherently stupid. And so in my teaching I have also come to encourage the self-development aspects of Wing Chun that are there just below the surface in things like chi-sau.

"When we strive to remove violent intent from chi-sau we are able to really study the structure of our own bodies and reactions, without getting distracted by striving to hit each other. This can deepen our understanding of the system and of ourselves.

"Then, when we become more experienced, we can introduce strikes, but without judging thoughts; using the feeling to react or take opportunities when they arise or set-up an opportunity ourselves by understanding our partner/opponent. All this of course depends on our own experiences; being patient; seeing things with a beginner's mind; trusting ourselves; not striving; accepting things as they actually are—not as we would wish them; and letting go of our thoughts. I have found this approach to the forms and exercises of Wing Chun, including chi-sau, to have been very successful in opening up the deeper undercurrents of the system.

"This is what makes Wing Chun a useful art even into one's old age. Ip Man, for example, in his later life in Hong Kong did not engage in fights. But the system was rich enough and deep enough to be relevant even in later life. This is a far cry from the more crude modern fighting systems coming about.

"Of course Wing Chun works extremely well in a fighting situation–but there's so much more to it than that. The system is wonderfully clever and fighters are not the only people who can benefit from it. We can use Wing Chun to hack away at our own stupidity, leaving us as intelligent as were meant to be before our families, friends, schoolteachers, the media, and the like got in the way.

Some of my students have told me that by training in Wing Chun they have been able to develop enough self-control to avoid stupid fights or get caught up in winning fights. They have learnt how to keep their tempers and their egos in check. Their knowledge of potentially lethal techniques has given them a sense of responsibility that they lacked beforehand. Meanwhile other students have found the ability to improvise under pressure has helped them in street violence.

"I believe that Nino and Wong used Wing Chun primarily as a fighting system which had some unspoken self-development benefits. Sifu Wong was already a fighter when he met Ip Man. Nino was already a fighter when he met Wong! But for both of them, Wing Chun took their fighting skills to a completely different level.

"I do not believe this is a new way of looking at Wing Chun. However, some teachers (especially in modern times) have changed things in order to take advantage of innocent and naive people. How different is this interpretation from what I was taught? Not different at all! Except that this is my expression of Wing Chun Kuen Kung-fu."

PART THREE
UP CLOSE

The Teachings of Sifu Loukas Kastrounis

In Part Three we take a look at some of the teachings of Sifu Loukas collated from his lessons, anecdotes, seminars, and instructions to students. Here his oral teachings and instructions are expanded on and embellished by references to other sources and the reader's attention is drawn to the wider implications hinted at in Loukas's deceptively straightforward statements. There is much to learn from this section of the book and we hope that the reader and practitioner will find that these chapters prove to be an invaluable resource and companion on their own personal Wing Chun journey.

8

MASTER CLASS 1
Training to Fight Without Fighting

"Therefore those who win every battle are not really skillful—those who render others' armies helpless without fighting are the best of all."

—Sun Tzu, *The Art of War*[22]

When you see Wing Chun being practiced it doesn't look like fighting. It is a mistake to think too much about fighting when you are practicing Wing Chun. The secrets of this art are in its forms. When the forms become second nature to you and you understand their significance, then you come to realize Wing Chun's potential in a fighting situation. In other words, although working with the forms and practicing Wing Chun will definitely make you capable of dealing with a fighting situation competently, if you are only thinking of fighting while practicing and learning Wing Chun, you will not absorb what the forms are meant to teach you. You have to look beyond fighting techniques in order to really gain the benefits from Wing Chun, even in a situation of confrontation.

But make no mistake about it. Wing Chun is a fighting system. But before we can talk about fighting we have to develop the correct mental condition—the right state of mind. And this cannot be bought. Paying your fees and attending class is not enough to develop this state of mind. Moreover the state of mind is not purely "intellectual." We are not talking here about rational thought processes. Ultimately what is needed is for the body to absorb the principles of Wing Chun so that they become natural responses in any given situation. This is what is meant when we say, *feel, don't think*. Bruce Lee was famous for saying this. Most people just think it's a cliché and don't realize what he meant. A Wing Chun practitioner should come to understand this and strive for it.

You cannot simply "learn" Wing Chun like you might learn a fact at school. You have to think of Wing Chun as a game. You "play" Wing Chun. When you think of learning some-

---

22. Thomas Cleary, tr., *The Art of War* (Boston: Shambhala, 1999), 90.

thing your brain takes the lead and this paradoxically gets in the way of your real learning. Of course the teacher has to speak to your rational faculties when he teaches. That is to say when a teacher explains a concept to you, naturally your brain processes this information intellectually. The teacher will instruct you through speech and action. As you hear his words and observe his actions you have to understand one thing above all else: *it is not enough just to watch and listen.* The goal is to *absorb* the art of Wing Chun into your body so that it becomes natural to you. This is how young children learn—and that's why they are so good at learning so much so quickly. The famous Italian educator, Dr. Maria Montessori called this "the absorbent mind" and even wrote a book with the same title. The famous language teacher Michel Thomas developed his entire method of foreign language teaching around this concept. "The teacher can open the door," says Loukas. "But the student has to walk through and learn by making his own mistakes."

The aim is come to a stage where in any given situation your responses remain true to the principles of body mechanics codified in each of the forms. So that your actions and reactions are naturally those that come from many years of playing Wing Chun.

Beginners and advanced practitioners of Wing Chun are outwardly engaged in the same practice. The difference however is in their understanding and absorption of this practice. The late, great, time management and productivity guru Stephen Covey wrote: "Begin with the End in Mind." For the beginner and the senior student the end is the same: to act in the most efficient manner possible to neutralize a threat to one's centerline. This is only possible if, when you are training, you realize that the purpose of instruction is not to understand intellectually but rather to internalize the concepts mechanically.

In this sense Loukas talks about precision in one's training. Indeed this seems to be characteristic of the Wong Shun Leung lineage of Wing Chun instructors. A great deal of emphasis is placed on precision in one's movements. This is especially true for beginners; but even those who have been practicing for a long time have to revisit these essential elements constantly.

When two practitioners are "playing" Wing Chun together, they have to think of themselves as working on a collaborative project. Each one is a mirror for his partner. As he checks his own positioning and alignment, as he adjusts his body positioning to correct his own structure, he must also be sure to feedback to his partner what he senses may be wrong or right about his partner's structure, positioning, and adjustments.

Imagination is important here. Take for example the Wing Chun horse stance. This is one of the first things a beginner is introduced to. It is the foundation of the Siu Nim Tau form and is vitally important in the entire Wing Chun system. However, one does not practice sitting correctly in the horse stance in order to remain fixed in this stance in a real-life situation. The horse stance is rigid and static while real life is flowing, dynamic. In this sense you might say real-life is more like the interplay of two friends engaged in chi-sau—with the give-and-take and fluidity, not like the solitary practice of Siu Nim Tau performed in an unmoving horse stance. But the static horse stance has a purpose—many purposes in fact—that become apparent with the patience and careful guidance of a good teacher.

One of these purposes is to help the body feel the optimum position for its own center of gravity. In other words you must understand where your optimum balance is when you are at rest—not understand this intellectually but rather instinctively so that in the midst of the dynamic situation of a conflict you are able to respond naturally and effortlessly settle into the most mechanically efficient state of rest given the requirements of the situation. It is because of the "requirements of the situation" that imagination becomes such a crucial element in the daily practice of Wing Chun within the artificial confines of the training hall amongst friends. The objective is not to become a slave to the system but rather in the end to make the system work for you.

Every time we come to our Wing Chun class we begin by practicing the first form. This "religious" dedication to our form and our training routines is important—it is even necessary. However, there is a danger in this devoted practice that we forget the purpose of what we are doing; and that we lose the natural fluidity and spontaneity that Wing Chun demands, ultimately, from the competent practitioner. Because, in the final analysis, this fluidity and naturalness is what a real life situation will inevitably require from us, if we are to survive and to be victorious.

The forms are there to serve you. You are not here to serve the form. *How?* First, understand the concepts of what you are practicing. Second, do not be under the illusion that immobility of the lower body coupled with the many movements of the hands and arms in the first form means there is no footwork in Siu Nim Tau. All those movements of the hands do not mean you are not practicing footwork in Siu Nim Tau. Although the lower body appears to be static you must realize that the Wing Chun footwork is also embodied in the very first form. It takes lots of hours of practice and self-reflection to discover this truth. But this raises an important question: *if this cannot be felt by the relatively inexperienced practitioner how can it at least be understood intellectually so that one knows what to look out for?*

In Wing Chun a kick is the same as a step in the sense that when the Wing Chun practitioner kicks he lands one step closer to the opponent—he does not kick and step back. By contrast, in other martial arts it is typical to kick and then retract to the position from where the kick originally came. This develops a "thief" mentality: stepping in with a punch and running back, stepping in with a kick and then moving back as quickly as possible to avoid getting hit. As is if you are trying to steal a shot and then run away to safety. The fixed horse-stance position of Siu Nim Tau is training your lower body to behave differently. The Wing Chun footwork that we want to develop here is to return to a firm grounded structure after a punch or kick but not a return to our previous location. Wing Chun encourages forward-moving energy or "spring-loaded forward moving energy": every kick becomes a step forward closing the distance between you and your opponent and so neutralizing the threat.

If you hit and run you have not necessarily neutralized the threat—you have most probably increased the likelihood of a strike back and also have probably aggravated the threat by angering your opponent. The brain says, "I want to hit, but I don't want to get hit. Let me hit the other guy and run away before he can hit me!" If you are lucky you might just hurt the other person enough to end the fight. But if you are unlucky—and this is more probable—you will have given strong incentives for your opponent to step in and hit you. The result is an ugly brutish exchange of blows and injuries—the very thing you were trying to avoid in the first place. This sort of fight is demonstrated well in sports like boxing and so called "mixed martial arts" competitions where opponents stand "toe to toe" and exchange blows and bruises. There is little art in such fighting and much less sense.[23]

When beginners in Wing Chun stand in the fixed horse stance, sinking their body, finding their center of gravity, locking their lower body, and moving their hands they are taking their first *steps* towards understanding Wing Chun footwork. (If you sense the word-play in this, then you have a feeling for Wing Chun.)

The more time beginners spend with this form the more their focus and perspective will come to change. As they develop in their practice they will come to learn about *Lat Sau Ching Chong* (forward spring-loaded energy) and about *choi ma/soi ma*. This will seep into their practice of the apparently static Siu Nim Tau form. In time the body begins to absorb new habits of movement. And they will come to see how the hands and upper body work in unison with the lower body. They will come to see, or rather "feel," how to move the lower body structure (tripod) in conjunction with the upper body fixed elbow position of the arms and all the other structural components in the most optimum way in order to achieve the following:

1. Protect their centerline
2. Disturb the opponent's centerline
3. And return or recover to the position of optimum stability

All this is honed and developed through what appears to be the "static" training of the lower body in Siu Nim Tau. When this has been achieved the result is that your entire being moves as a whole, and you move forward not in order to run back again, but rather to advance and gain ground against the enemy.

One of the great joys of Wing Chun practice is this deeply entrenched unity in every single movement of every single form in the entire system. This unity is a treasure that reveals to the thinking practitioner a great deal about themselves. It takes time to discover these treasures of self-realization as they are so completely integrated into Wing Chun's hidden subtleties. Most people do not have the inclination or the patience to ever be able to savor this level of perfection.

---

23. With this in mind it is well and proper to call Wing Chun a martial art, although Loukas, like Wong Shung Leung before him, prefers to use the term "martial skills." When they say Wing Chun is martial skills as opposed to martial art they wish to emphasize the technical and precise nature of Wing Chun and that it is not interested in aesthetics. And yet when others say it is a martial art they wish to emphasize that it is more profound and deeper than mere technical precision. In the Japanese tradition this understanding is encapsulated in the terms *do* (meaning "way") and *jutsu* (meaning "technique").

Unfortunately many teachers become disillusioned with the impatience of their students and give up trying to impart this level of precision to their pupils. More often than not, as time passes and Wing Chun grows in popularity this real essence of Wing Chun is becoming lost—diminishing the quality and reputation of the art.

In the end mastery in any art comes from the joy of practicing it throughout one's life. Eventually the practice becomes a part of oneself—it both instructs the practitioner and is informed by the practitioner's experiences. In this way the art itself is enriched and and is (hopefully) passed down through the generations. This is what has happened with Wing Chun and with other arts—both martial arts and arts from other disciplines. And yet there are many more arts and traditions that have not lived on and others that are dying a slow death in our very own times.

Let us take what we have said so far to another level of subtlety in order to illuminate how rich and fulfilling the practice of Wing Chun can be and demonstrate how it can be instructive in other areas of life. We have said that the practitioner should not be under the illusion that the emphasis on keeping the positions of the lower body fixed in the horse stance (such as in Siu Nim Tau) means he is not training footwork at this stage. Rather as we have explained, although ultimately it can only be appreciated through practice, the stillness of the lower body is precisely early training for correct footwork. We have said that Wing Chun requires us to move the whole body forward with a kick or step and narrow the distance between our opponent and ourselves. There are strategic and philosophical implications to this which often only come as insights to practitioners after many years of devotion to the art. One of these is the essential truth that Wing Chun teaches us through this principle: namely, that in order to neutralize a threat properly you must come closer to the enemy not move away from him. And moreover you have to commit your entire person to drawing closer to your opponent—it cannot be a half-hearted commitment. You have to literally narrow the distance between your opponent and yourself by committing yourself to moving closer to him in a hostile situation rather than moving away and increasing the distance. If you have a "tit-for-tat" mentality—hit him and then run—he will also hit you and run. You will end up exchanging blows in a terrible war of attrition where no one is the winner. Does this sound familiar? Think about the great turmoil, warfare, and conflicts that afflicted China as it came into modernity and that we described earlier in this book. The violent and turbulent world Ip Man was born into, and the era of tyranny and rebellion that was the catalyst for Wing Chun itself. Think about the wars and conflicts in our own time.

The only hope for an end to these types of violence are the people on both sides of that divide that are trying to bridge the distance by coming closer to each other through efforts of peace and conciliation. It takes courage to be able to do that. It also takes a deep sense of rootedness and grounding. A sense of personal stability and equilibrium—of knowing and feeling one's own "center of gravity," one's rootedness and being able to take that stability with you even as you step forward. It takes being stable enough in your own identity to be able to step forward with softness and a lack of aggression. If the other side does not respond to this softness in kind but rather maintains a state of belligerence, your stability will lead them to succumb to the momentum of their own aggression. But this requires a raw honesty that is hard for most people to realize.

This thinking can be applied to any situation of conflict—personal, professional, with a spouse or family member, with a friend or colleague. But it takes years of cultivating stability in oneself and of being critically self-examining before a person can develop this level of honesty and courage. As students train in the Wing Chun schools of Sifu Loukas dotted around the world you start to notice elements of this emerge in them: slowly at first and then—as they practice drills together regularly—you hear student exchanges like: "I noticed you didn't have your arm quite high enough, but hey, I make that mistake myself all the time" or "…well we're all beginners here I'm still learning that myself…" and "if you see me get it wrong go ahead and correct me…" This is just one of the esoteric gems hidden in the practice of Wing Chun. But for many of us it is a truth that we will never have the fortitude to realize.

In military strategy the same principle applies. To bring the threat to an end one attempts to gain as much ground as possible and then embed one's forces to hold the territory. The more rapidly one is able to gain ground and the more efficiently one is able to consolidate the gains and bring about stability, the more quickly and easily victory is obtained. The great Japanese swordsman Miyamoto Musashi hints at this when he writes:

> *In martial arts, in the midst of battle, it is also essential to "cross the ford." Sensing the state of opponents, aware of your own mastery, you cross the ford by means of the appropriate principles, just as a skilled captain goes over a sea-lane.*
>
> *Having crossed over the ford, furthermore, there is peace of mind.*
>
> *To "cross a ford," put the adversary in a weak position and get the jump yourself; then you will quickly prevail whether in large-scale military science or individual martial-arts; the sense of crossing a ford is essential. It should be savored thoroughly.*[24]

The astute practitioner of Wing Chun can see the truth of Musashi's words in his own practice: we might say "awareness of your own mastery" is awareness of one's own center of gravity and balance (honed through the "static" lower body training in Siu Nim Tau); "crossing the ford by means of the appropriate principle" for Wing Chun would mean by means of the "lines" or bridges presented by the opponent's own movements and position of hands; "put the adversary in a weak position and get the jump yourself," or in other words disturb the opponent's centerline and move in yourself to close the gap—for example, by kicking and stepping forward along the lines presented by the opponent and trained through correct body alignment. "Having crossed the ford there is peace of mind" because after having moved one regains stability by intuitively returning to the equilibrium trained in Siu Nim Tau and other Wing Chun concepts. One's centerline is facing the opponent; the gap has been closed—neutralizing the opponent's threat, and ideally his centerline is off balance. All this comes from understanding rootedness, not intel-

---

24. Thomas Cleary, tr., *The Illustrated Book of Five Rings* (Trumble, CT: Weatherhill, 1993), 51.

lectually but through feeling it following regular hours of practice and through reflecting over the deeper implications of that practice.

In Wing Chun we are learning simple principles with profound implications. The first of these is to step in toward the opponent. But this is precisely where the fear of getting hurt lies because you are required to get closer to the source of the threat rather than move away from it. In order to resolve this, one needs to have the correct alignment of upper and lower body. Next is to understand shifting (*yoi ma*); "moving your stance forward/moving your stance back (*choi ma/soi ma*); and *yo ma*—using the hips to move the direction of the spine, not the feet. "All this is preparation or conditioning of the body for Wing Chun proper," Loukas reminds us. "Now you are preparing yourself to be able to do Wing Chun."

*

UNDER PRESSURE IN CHI-SAU

"So the rule of military operations is not to count on opponents not coming, but to rely on having ways of dealing with them; not to count on opponents not attacking, but to rely on having what cannot be attacked."
—Sun Tzu, *The Art of War*[25]

I'm not thinking about hitting in chi-sau even under pressure—that's a common mistake. What I'm thinking about is not being hit. If we suddenly freeze in the middle of chi-sau and look at our opponent we will notice different angles of shots that they have at us. If we ask our opponent he may be able to explain other shots that we didn't think about or notice.

When you only see your own shot you are missing the most important thing—where *you* will be hit. And that is what Wing Chun is about—seeing the lines and the nearest target that these lines will take you to naturally and effortlessly, but also seeing the lines that you have opened up for the opponent to hit you. (This is where the counterattacking element of Wing Chun becomes clear, emphasizing it is a counterattack system.) This is completely different from the "tit-for-tat," "I hit you, you hit me" mentality of sparring commonly found in other martial arts or sports-like mentalities in training. Here in chi-sau we are trying to develop natural instinctive feelings for openings into our opponent while closing and removing any openings for our opponent. We are not exchanging blows but rather exchanging notes, developing a natural sense of movement that is mechanically efficient and as effortless as possible while also being safe.

---

25. Thomas Cleary, tr., *The Illustrated Art of War* (Boston: Shambhala, 1998), 168.

But because of insecurity you are thinking about how to hit when doing chi-sau. A useful point is to try and reverse this psychology when training and think, "How can I minimize the number of times I am hit while I am hitting?" Be careful! Wing Chun is efficient and precise. It is mechanically, one might even say physiologically, perfect. But we as human beings are not perfect. Can you accept that?

Fighting is not choreography. In fighting there is punching, kicking, and biting. There are "no holds barred." The question is when in a fight can you control your emotions—your anger, your rage, your fear, your insecurities—and instead focus on what you should be protecting, which are your stability, your movements?

Figure 8-1. "If I can hit him, he can hit me too." Here the game is to avoid each other's pointing finger (indicating a clear path to a strike).

As the illustration shows, Sifu has two hits on Nick, and Nick has one on Sifu. Sifu is better off, but he should not take the risk of being hit by Nick. You don't want to attack while the opponent's finger is pointing directly through a clear line to you. Sifu will not attack until he has avoided Nick's other hand. This is the intelligent game of chi-sau: to hit without being hit. Requiring combat skills and strategy, this is a game of both mental and physical aptitude. (See also Chapter 9 below for more on the "Mexican Standoff.")

Sometimes the distance is such that you cannot hit the opponent and he cannot hit you. In the game of chi-sau you may choose to provoke or invite your partner by presenting them a clear line along which to attack you. But if you do this be sure to be ready for that attack. Don't look at your hands—see the whole picture. In other words avoid the other hand and feel through your body's structure. That is the essence of Wing Chun.

In the words of Sun Tzu:

Therefore you make their route a long one, luring them on in hopes of gain. When you set out after others and arrive before them, you know the strategy of making the distance near.[26]

*

FORWARD PUNCHES AND LAP-SAU

Use the forms to be able to understand centerline, center of gravity, forward energies, structure, posture and body mechanics. In this sense, forms in Wing Chun are very different to forms or katas in other martial arts where the focus is on drilling techniques within the form. In Wing Chun the forms are not so much about set techniques but rather a means of training the body and mind to maintain correct alignment and positioning.

Let us examine, for example, the forward punches in Siu Nim Tau. When practicing the punches, first think about sinking the elbows or "sinking the bridge." Do not bring your elbow too far back after punching but focus instead of "sinking" the elbow. Usually we talk about "bridges" from the second form (Chum Kiu) onward. But we can also think about bridges in Siu Nim Tau: drop the elbow ("sink the bridge") and punch from the elbow, extending the forearm ("cross the bridge"). Moreover, we never want to punch twice (consecutively) with the same hand: always punch with the other hand. With this in mind, we can start practicing an exercise to develop punching that reinforces our practice of Siu Nim Tau and what it teaches us while helping us to understand it better at the same time.

Start off slow and then gradually increase the speed. Use your imagination. Think of different opponents and dynamically changing situations—now an opponent is in front of you, now they are coming from the side—so shift your body. Now they are coming too fast, so step back and sink the bridge to receive and then immediately step forward with the structure as you continue punching. Remember: if you need to step back to make the space do so, immediately step forward afterward.

As you move and punch in this manner be mindful of posture, shifting, stepping, and checking to make sure your structure is maintained as much as possible. As you "shadow box" in this way ask yourself constantly:

1. Is my rear foot pointing in the direction I am going?
2. Is my front foot turned in appropriately?
3. Is my spine straight and am I being careful not to bob up and down as I move?
4. As I punch, am I thinking about bridges—crossing the bridge, sinking the bridge?
5. When I shift to change direction, am I shifting with my whole body or just my hands?

---

26. Ibid., 150.

Another way to develop correct punching with body structure and footwork is to practice with a partner. Have the partner throw different punches at you while you move in with the forward punches. Think of Siu Nim Tau, but make no mistake—in Wing Chun you do not fight like this. This is only in films. If you fight like this in real life you will get beaten up. This is only to teach you one concept: just punch! And punch many times—without chasing hands, without trying to see or wait for what happens.

If I think about deflecting, blocking, and then punching, the opponent has time for the next kick, punch, head butt, or strike. This isn't so much about punching directly from the centerline in an upright position. In a real fight that won't often be possible. But the conditioning gained through straight punching properly will mean that you punch correctly—not from your shoulder, but driving your punch through your elbows powered by your structure in a direct line of attack opened up by the opponents movements and positioning. Remember the Wing Chun punch is like a piston. It is "charged" when you sink the elbow and it fires when you drive through the elbow with the hips and the structure. This is the punch—like it or not, that's all that is needed for punching properly if the body has been conditioned in the right way.

Once you are comfortable with your partner throwing punches at you and you feel you are responding appropriately with the forward punches, footwork, and structure, you can add

Figure 8-2. "Be mindful of your opponent's other hand." Here Sifu Loukas demonstrates that it is not his left hand that Nick needs to worry about, but rather his right hand. A novice in Nick's position may think he has the situation under control because he has dealt with the initial attack. But Sifu Loukas draws Nick's attention to his incoming right hand, pointing to illustrate the danger and the line of attack.

another level of practice by introducing lap-sau. As your partner throws punches, move correctly and see if you can execute a lap-sau. But be mindful of your opponent's other hand (Figure 8-2).

There are all kinds of lap-sau, so do not think narrowly. A lap-sau can be performed behind the neck or from the shoulder blades or even from the opponent's belt—whatever is nearest and can be "hooked." The important things are timing, sinking the elbows, and being mindful of the opponent's hand and strategy.

Lap-sau can be performed on many "targets" and can then lead to controlling the opponent and ending the fight.

There's nothing wrong with a lap to the neck. But when doing the lap-sau be sure to avoid the other hand (see Figure 6-23 above). Wing Chun is about strategy not techniques. When I lap I don't do so for the sake of doing a lap-sau. I'm not becoming a slave of the form or technique. I lap-sau for a purpose.

But sometimes my first lap-sau will work but my partner's response makes the following technique not work. There is no need to force the next technique. We want to flow. That is what Siu Nim Tau is teaching us. Flow from one technique to the next, to the next: don't become part of the problem. Be part of the solution. If the second lap-sau will not work because of how your partner has responded then try something else. We might say, "Look for the lap and make it work for you." Or we might say: "Be part of the solution—avoid the other hand."

Figure 8-3. "There's nothing wrong with a lap-sau to the neck." Notice Sifu's elbow position.

Visual Cues: Forward Punches and Lap-Sau

"Be part of the solution, not part of the problem."
As Nick comes in with his right, Sifu Loukas executes a lap-sau sending Nick off balance along the trajectory of his own momentum. At the same time a subtle shift positions Loukas in just the right place to end the fight while his left hand lands the finishing blow. Due to body mechanics and momentum Nick's left hand is no longer in a position to cause any harm. Loukas tells his students: "Now I am the one with all the shots. Be part of the solution, not part of the problem."

Figure 8-4

Figure 8-5

Figure 8-6

Figure 8-7

Figure 8-8

9

MASTER CLASS 2

Avoiding the Mexican Stand-Off
(Chi-Sau And Developing Forward Spring-Loaded Energy)

"The great mistake is to anticipate the outcome of the engagement; you ought not to be thinking of whether it ends in victory or defeat. Let nature take its course, and your tools will strike at the right moment."

—*Bruce Lee*

When doing chi-sau it is important to offer the opponent/partner energy. This is critical. Imagine two boxers trying to train together to improve their skills. If they square up facing each other in their guards but do not offer each other a threat, they won't learn from each other. The point is not to be aggressive but to offer your partner something to play with or, if you like, work from.

For example a common mistake is to assume a fook-sau hand position that offers no forward energy. This habit can develop from an incorrect practice of single-hand drills.

Figure 9-1. Incorrect fook-sau. Here, Nick's fook-sau lacks energy.

Figure 9-2. Sifu Loukas corrects Nick's fook-sau.

Figure 9-3. Correct fook-sau position. "Now the partner has something to play with as the fook-sau energy is moving forward."

This feeling is important for cultivation of lat sau chi chung—or forward spring-loaded energy. So when you train try to cultivate this energy. Its essence is embedded in the repeated emphasis on forward punching, on structure and correct alignment of arms with the upper and lower body. All of this encourages simple, direct, forward energies.

Before you touch your partner's hand you can experiment with him to see if he is "connected." If your partner assumes a tan-sau, test the connection by applying a gentle force along his arm. If your partner is connected—if his arm is aligned correctly—the force will transfer along his arm, through his hips down to his feet. The natural response will be that his foot will step backward and his entire structure will move accordingly.

Figure 9-4

Figure 9-5

Figures 9-4 through 9-9. Testing the correct alignment in tan-sau to see if your partner is connected. Nick tests Sifu Loukas's "connection" by applying forward pressure through his tan-sau palm. The energy from Nick's forward pressure channels naturally into Sifu's tan-sau palm and

Figure 9-6

Figure 9-7

through his body structure, resulting in Sifu's backward movement. Note that Sifu Loukas and Nick both maintain body structure and alignment throughout the exercise. When both partners are able to receive each other's energies in a such an effortless way, chi-sau practice is possible.

Figure 9-8

Figure 9-9

This means that his tan-sau arm is forming a bridge from his lower body up to his hands. Your partner should not move back deliberately. Instead, he should be relaxed and let the momentum of the force travelling through his bridge arm into the structure move him naturally. If the tan-sau is not correctly aligned his body will not respond naturally to that force in this way. But if the bridge arm structure is in place, then it means that, conversely, the force from his structure can travel through that arm and be transferred, if necessary to his opponent/partner. For example, if the partner's arm is aligned to his shoulder the force you apply will cause his shoulder to move, not his lower body. This is a typical problem with beginners as most people are used to engaging their upper-body strength rather than keeping their shoulders relaxed.

Figure 9-10　　　　　　　　　　　　　Figure 9-11

"An improper bridge arm will eventually cause injury to your shoulder and does not allow your partner to learn anything from you." Sifu Loukas points out the correct alignment of the tan-sau bridge arm. Notice the relative position of the hands and elbows.

This is important because (among other things):
1. Improper alignment can cause injury (such as when you repeatedly apply force, which could eventually lead to a damaged spine or dislocated shoulder).
2. If your partner's tan-sau is not aligned correctly you cannot learn anything beneficial from their hand when practicing.
3. Only if both your and your partner's hands are aligned properly with the rest of the structure will you both have spring-loaded energy and therefore be able to obtain the correct exchange of energies to learn effectively from each other.

All of the above applies to the fook-sau and bong-sau shapes too.

Once both partners are able to form correct bridges they can start "playing" or "practicing" in order to internalize the principles by absorbing the correct feelings.

Figure 9-12. "Both have bridges. There is the danger."

Look at the illustration above. We now have two bridges. "Unfortunately for Nick," says Sifu, "his bridges are pointing to my side while my bridges are pointing at his centerline. I don't want to be in front of him. This is one of the biggest mistakes people make when learning Wing Chun. Both players end up facing each other in a sort of "Mexican stand-off."

Figure 9-13. A Mexican Stand-off is a confrontation amongst two or more parties in which no participant can proceed or retreat without being exposed to danger. As a result, all participants need to maintain the strategic tension which remains unresolved until some outside event makes it possible to resolve it. (*Mexican Standoff* by Martin SoulStealer/Wikimedia Commons/Public Domain.)

The "outside event" that is needed to resolve this awkward predicament is where "the game" of Wing Chun is played out. And its beauty is expressed. And its genius demonstrated. This outside event comes from "feeling" the energies of your opponent through your structure, sensing his tension, and being awake to the emptiness that comes from a gap that opens up in the interaction of chi-sau. Like a conversation or a dialogue—an exchange of questions and answers takes place between opponents. Loukas reminds us to ask intelligent questions not stupid ones. The answer to the "questions" your opponent asks (in the shape of a fook-sau, or tan-sau or a punch or kick or anything else) does not come from guess work or over-thinking and calculation. Rather, it comes from feeling—the feeling of a loaded spring suddenly released into emptiness because of your opponent's actions heading toward his centerline along a path described by the opponent's own "bridges." That spring is powered from the lower body not the upper body, and upon impact it returns like a bamboo to its reset position while at the same time the other hand has taken its place.

The Chess Game of Wing Chun

The following sequence of illustrations seeks to highlight the unfolding of the skills, body mechanics, strategy, art, and expression of Wing Chun in action as Sifu Loukas and Nick touch hands. Note how all of the details we have examined so far come into play here.

Figure 9-14. Nick has executed a bong-sau to divert Sifu's punch.
But here Nick is over-leaning and his structure has been disturbed which means he will struggle to recover his structure to respond to the next strike. Bong-sau is a throwing technique but here Nick has destabilized his structure, and so his bong-sau is not correct either. In a sense, instead of throwing Sifu he is throwing himself. Every technique in Wing chun is designed to disturb the opponent's structure. Here he has disturbed his own structure not his opponent's, and so he is vulnerable to the next hit coming from Sifu.

Figure 9-15. Nick attempts to divert Sifu's left hand with a tan-sau.
"We are testing here the tan-sau technique and how it can be applied." Nick wants to divert Sifu's left hand away from his body, but again Nick is leaning forward. This means that even though his tan-sau might succeed in diverting one of Sifu's hands away, his poor structure means that Nick may not be able to resist any force being applied by Sifu (such as a punch, a push, a pull from a lap-sau, or any other force). Nick's forward-leaning body means that any force Sifu applies cannot be absorbed by his structure.

Figure 9-16. "Nick is in danger!"
Sifu points the finger of his right hand to indicate a clear line of attack towards Nick. Nick is in danger here because he didn't execute a punch with his free hand at the same time as executing the tan-sau. This is why Wing Chun can be understood correctly as a counterattack system.

The mistakes here and above:
1. Nick is leaning and so has disturbed his own structure.
2. He is not punching simultaneously with the tan-sau. Loukas explains: "Nick is playing defensively—this is a typical mistake. The other hand should be punching. As it is pictured here it is doing nothing. Actually, in movies it is often portrayed in this wrong manner."
3. Nick's tan-sau is not strong because it is not supported by Nick's lower body but by his shoulder. The shoulder is not designed to support the tan-sau so there is the possibility of injury due to the use of improper body mechanics.

Figure 9-17 "Tell me how you would like to be hit."
Sifu has now disengaged his left hand from Nick's contact by shifting his own position and his right hand is already loaded for the next attack (the pointing finger). Nick has shifted too much toward his right side as he chased Sifu's left hand. By disengaging his hand Sifu now has two hands ready to strike Nick. Nick has exposed himself to being hit from both of Sifu's hands. Sifu points out: "Here is an example of the opponent telling you how he would like to be hit. This is why sensitivity and shifting are practiced so much." Nick has to shift to realign himself in order to hit Sifu. But as he does that he risks automatically walking into Sifu's right punch. It's as if Sifu is asking Nick: "Tell me how you would like to be hit." Your opponent's mistakes will answer that question for you. The defensive moves from Nick (represented in all the sequence so far) are not offering any threat, which means it's just a matter of time before he will be hit. The best defense is offense.

Figure 9-18. Nick is now offering a threat but he is directly facing Sifu.
Now we have a situation where there is the possibility of an exchange of punches (a "Mexican stand-off"). To correct this, Nick needs to shift his centerline away from Sifu to be safe while he is attacking. Redirecting one's own centerline slightly off from the opponent's threat is like making oneself invisible to the opponent's attack. Wong Shun Leung was fond of telling his students, "If you cannot become invisible, learn Wing Chun. It's the next best thing!"

As the body shifts correctly it generates further acceleration that translates into more force in the attack (f=ma).

Also notice that while Nick's tan-sau is correctly extended to intercept Sifu's left hand, Nick's punching arm is not extended correctly to be able to punch. Nick's tan-sau is "chasing" Sifu's hand and his punch is not effective. In reality, Nick is waiting to be hit while he has given himself a false sense of security. He may think his left hand is ready to punch but actually his punch has collapsed. His defensive play means he is not offering any threat even though he may think he is. Again, he is waiting to be hit.

Figure 9-19. Nick puts Sifu in danger!
Nick corrects his mistakes by shifting appropriately, regaining his structure. Here we can see that Nick's body mechanics are now aligned optimally. He is offering a threat with both his hands and has placed Sifu in danger.

In the following sequence of illustrations you can see the chess game of Wing Chun in action. But there is one crucial difference: in combat there is no time to think. The correct body mechanics have to be trained to respond instinctively under the frightening situation of a real conflict.

Figure 9-20

Figure 9-21

Nick continues his threat.
Nick has shifted his body to the right and has opened a line for a punch to Sifu's center—receiving and diverting the incoming attack, taking away the threat from Sifu, and offering a threat of his own with an additional possibility of a second strike with his right hand. All he needs to do now is close the bridge by stepping in.
Note: In the middle of the sequence (Figure 9-21) Sifu indicates the danger Nick is in by pointing with his finger. If Nick stops at this point and does not continue shifting there is a real possibility of

Figure 9-22

Figure 9-23

a "clash of fists" (Sifu's right hand with Nick's left hand). However, Nick continues the movement to avoid this danger as already indicated.

Also notice here a very subtle point: this sequence shows how tan-sau can be used within a "triangle" framework against a circular attack. This has to be considered carefully. There are so many subtleties here that it is difficult to grasp without dedicated practice. (Only some of these subtleties are captured in the illustrations—none of which are identical although they may appear to be so at first glance.)

Figure 9-24

Sifu regains the advantage but is not out of danger.
Sifu Loukas shifts in order to avoid Nick's threats and give himself a direct attack. He does this by following a "triangular" motion along with his tan-sau and keeping his rear hand ready to punch. However, Sifu is vulnerable here to Nick's elbow. If Nick raises the elbow of his right hand he can strike Sifu's knuckles (Figure 9-24). Also Sifu's tan-sau has not yet trapped (or immobilized) Nick's other hand (Figure 9-26).

9: MASTER CLASS 2   137

Figure 9-25

Figure 9-26

Figure 9-27

Sifu checkmates Nick!
By stepping in along the line of an imaginary triangle Sifu continues his movement, immobilizing Nick's elbow and therefore controlling the arm while simultaneously striking with his left punch. Notice that Sifu's *tan-sau* is extending toward Nick's left shoulder. By the end of this sequence Nick's elbow is trapped, Sifu's fist is in Nick's ribs, and he is off balance. To regain his balance he would have to turn toward Sifu's next punch, giving Sifu opportunities for further attacks—a strike, a throw, or other take downs. In other words, from this position Nick has no opportunity to recover. The game is over!

Figure 9-28

Figure 9-29

10

MASTER CLASS 3

"No Technique as Technique"

(Chum Kiu Concepts, The Beginner Mind, And Self-Discovery)

"The person who says it cannot be done should not interrupt the person doing it."
—*Chinese Proverb*

It is not uncommon for beginners to do things in chi-sau without understanding the full meaning of what they are doing. The meaning becomes clearer and the understanding grows with practice. Imagine if you are engaged in chi-sau with someone and in the course of the quick-paced exchanges they perform what looks to you like a very bad lap-sau. You remember your teacher telling you not to lap-sau like that. You should not stop your chi-sau practice and point out to your partner that their lap-sau was wrong—even if you have the best of intentions. Because it was not in fact a lap-sau; it was a lan-sau (a lifting block, bridging or deflection technique)! And if it worked in the spontaneous situation arising from the dynamic interplay of chi-sau, then all the better—there is something for both of you to learn from that. Chi-sau allows you to experiment in a controlled environment where you are under pressure and subject to uncertainty: two factors that are ever present in all confrontations.

Now imagine as a beginner you execute this lan-sau. You have never heard of lan-sau. Perhaps in your mind you are doing lap-sau. Perhaps you think to yourself, "That was a rubbish lap-sau." Better not to think too much. In the words of Bruce Lee, "Feeeel! Don't think!" Be natural and learn from the doing. Don't worry too much about this technique or that technique, whether your bong-sau was correct or your lap-sau was proper. As a beginner you may not realize exactly what you are doing, but so long as you adhere to the basic principles, body structure, alignment, and efficiency of Wing Chun, and so long as what you are doing works—then that's all that matters. What more could you ask for?

So it depends on your understanding. We cannot say in chi-sau, "Excuse me that is wrong! You're not allowed to do that." The system is open for exchange of ideas and practice. And so beginners can train with more experienced practitioners and each can benefit from the other by keeping an open mind.

In the following sequences and accompanying commentary we seek to help you glimpse some of these finer points of Wing Chun. The sequences have been chosen carefully to demonstrate the principles already outlined and to reveal deeper layers of Wing Chun including its versatility as a fighting art that includes not only striking and kicking but also grappling.

Visual Cues: "The One Who Hits Last Gets to Go Home"

Figure 10-1

Figure 10-2

Nick executes a bong-sau to deflect Sifu's attack.
Nick pivots simultaneously with his bong-sau in reponse to Sifu's attack. Because bong-sau has to be used as a throwing technique this simultaneous pivoting is necessary. Notice how Sifu's body is thrown off his line of attack as a result.

Figure 10-3
Nick's bong-sau has been lifted too high.
Sifu has caused Nick's elbow to go above his shoulder making Nick vulnerable to being thrown down. Nick's structure is now broken and we can clearly see that he is in danger.

Figure 10-4   **Figure 10-5**
Sifu corrects Nick's structure by bringing the bong-sau into the correct position.
He then tests Nick's bong-sau by applying pressure to the elbow (Figure 10-5). If the structure is correct Nick's bong-sau will absorb the pressure, or alternatively Nick can step forward and move his elbow toward Sifu's centerline. Note that he has to step with his right leg (the same side as his bong-sau) in order to make this effective. If his structure is not correct he will not be able to do this.

Figure 10-6

Following the adjustments, Nick ends up in a position where he has avoided Sifu's other hand and he is not vulnerable to be hit by Sifu.
He has also set up Sifu to be able to counterattack his next strike. Often people think to stop a punch with bong-sau but actually bong-sau is a preparation to set up the next attack. Bong-sau is an intermediate phase to avoid the danger and set up the counterattack. It's not an attack in itself.

Figure 10-7

Figure 10-8

Figure 10-9. Sensing the danger, Sifu shifts and swaps hands while changing direction in order to avoid the other punch from Nick. But...

Figure 10-10 ...Nick counters with a tan-sau and punch, setting up Sifu and regaining the upper hand.

Nick has used economy of motion and direct simple counterattacks while Sifu has had to make large movements in order to try to strike Nick. But by doing that Sifu has made himself vulnerable to be hit and again ends up in a position from which he has no recovery. Nick can now continue rapid punches to Sifu.

Figure 10-11. Sifu Loukas emphasizes that you need to test your Wing Chun to see not only what works but also how to recover from difficult positions.

"Remember as we have said before: in Wing Chun we aim to hit last not hit first. The one who hits last gets to go home. Wing Chun training is based on counterattacks—Nick was late to hit but ended up being 'on time,' utilizing body mechanics, triangular paths of movement, and economy of motion."

Visual Cues: "Do Not Be Distracted by the Technique—The Technique Comes Last."

Figure 10-12. Sifu and Nick face off. The beginning of a confrontation.
Both can strike and it is not clear who will strike first. Note that Sifu's posture indicates he is subtly waiting for Nick to make his move. "Every action has a reaction."

(following page)
Nick offers the first attack.
Sifu takes his hand and slightly diverts his punch, but Nick remains just out of range for Sifu to make a counterattack. If Sifu steps closer he can be hit by Nick.
Sifu is acting behind Nick's rapid punches. He executes a bong-sau to avoid Nick's next punch. Sifu's bong-sau needs to "accelerate" in order for him to execute the next technique and gain the initiative. Here structure, body mechanics, timing, distance, accuracy, and finally technique all become crucial (but only in this order of priority). Do not be distracted by the technique—the technique comes last! Here the quality of single-hand training (tan chi-sau) takes on a real-life importance. Sifu needs to wait rather than rush in for an attack.

Figure 10-13

Figure 10-14

Figure 10-15. Sifu's ban-sau becomes a pulling technique.
Here we can see the importance of the correct understanding of chain punches—pull and push (or "pull and punch, pull and punch"). Without pull and push (lat-sau ching chun "spring loaded forward energy") it is not Wing Chun. Sifu Wong Shun Leung would emphasize this many times in his teachings. When there is emptiness we can strike. We do not strike when there is no emptiness.

"Here experience and strategy become paramount —not just technical knowledge of Wing Chun. Sifu Nino used to say that after one has completed the system and strategy has been honed deep within the body Wing Chun can be applied anywhere."

Figure 10-16. Sifu's pulling motion is designed to either apply a lock or send Nick crashing into the floor.

Alternatively, if Nick doesn't go all the way down Sifu's rear hand can take a clear shot at Nick. This is why the pulling motion of the rear hand is emphasized. It is the rear hand that is used for punching. The concentrated force generated by the combination of one hand pulling and the other hand striking creates maximum impact on the opponent. If Nick falsely believes he has a punch available against Sifu, his own motion will assist in making that impact even greater. Again, "the opponent will tell you how he would like to be hit." In summary, Sifu has three options for strikes while Nick has only one option—to go down. This is Wing Chun.

Visual Cues: "Two Hands Overcome One"—Multiple Simultaneous Activities

Figure 10-17

Figure 10-18

Bong-sau sets up Sifu to move his rear hand as efficiently as possible into an attacking motion. This enables Sifu to cross the bridge, use a pak-sau to restrain Nick's elbows to prevent him striking,

10: MASTER CLASS 3   153

Figure 10-19

Figure 10-20

and at the same time execute a strike to Nick's face (Figure 10-20). If the sequence were to continue Sifu has another strike from his rear hand, also a kick and takedown techniques (see below).

Figure 10-21. Alternative view.
Here you can clearly see how Sifu has switched hands, executed another pak-sau, and simultaneously executed another strike. At no moment in time throughout the entire sequence does Sifu allow Nick's hands to be unattended.

With an opponent only using one hand at a time to attack, he cannot cope with the two hands of the Wing Chun practitioner working simultaneously. The reality is such that Nick's one hand is contending with Sifu's two hands all of the time. Clearly in such a scenario the Wing Chun practitioner has the advantage.

Visual Cues: Look-Sau and Chi-Sau Drills

Figure 10-22. A common sight in Wing Chun—two people rolling hands—also known as look-sau or sticky hands.

This is practicing stillness while trying to maintain body structure and hand structure, and at the same time, feeling the other person's hands. Where are they? What are they doing (like pushing backward)?

The energy should be felt through your elbows and into your legs. Why? Because you are testing your structure and making sure you do not move backward or forward while taking away the threatening hands. (In this case the threatening hand is Nick's tan-sau, which Sifu is monitoring with his fook-sau and vice-versa for Nick—he is monitoring Sifu's bong-sau with his fook-sau). So both practitioners are simultaneously feeling, practicing, and making sure the lower body structure remains intact. This is not fighting per se, but practicing to improve sensitivity and getting comfortable with feeling the other persons hands and energy.

This is the beginning of learning to practice chi-sau.

Figure 10-23. A typical chi-sau drill exercise. Both Nick and Sifu must react to each other's hands. In this illustration we see Sifu performing a lap-sau with a *man-sau* ("asking hand"). Nick is responding with a *wu-sau* ("protecting hand"). In this instance Sifu is effectively testing the alertness of Nick's wu-sau.

Visual Cues: A Drill to Develop Chi-Sau and Combat Skills (Continuing Sequence from Above)

Figure 10-24

Figure 10-25

After the look-sau, Sifu and Nick continue their practice into a drill to develop combat skills (and by extension chi-sau skills).
To avoid Nick's direct attack, Sifu guides Nick's threatening hand away with a gan-sau while also striking at his ribs. Note that Sifu is not in front of Nick—effectively becoming "invisible" to Nick's threatening hand (here you see the importance of yoi-ma).

Figure 10-26

Figure 10-27

Before Nick can recover, Sifu has switched hands by monitoring Nick's elbow and executing another punch (Figure 10-27). Sifu then continues the attack with a lap-sau and elbow strike (Figure 10-28); following up with an armlock takedown technique (Figure 10-29).

Figure 10-28

Figure 10-29

"In real combat it is unlikely that the sequence will be exactly like this. You may only need one or other of these techniques or in a different sequence. But in order to train for combat, you need to drill exercises like this so that the mind and body can develop the reflexes and instincts to find its own correct response. This is important to remember: do not confuse chi-sau training for combat. It is not combat, but preparation for combat."

Visual Cues: "Your Body Weight Is Your Power"

In Figures 10-30 to 10-34, Sifu adjusts Nick's body structure. Initially, Nick is leaning backward, then he is leaning forward too much. After Sifu's adjustments, Nick's body structure is optimized with his center of gravity, and he can now move his entire body as one unit—ready to attack and receive an attack. He is able to move his structure comfortably in any direction without leaving behind any kind of link (such as an arm or leg).

When people attack they tend to lean forward (making it difficult to recover by going backward), or when they are defending they lean backward (making it difficult to recover from an attack). This is why Siu Nim Tau is based on stillness—to allow the practitioner to discover the correct body balance to move as a unit forward and backward. This is part of the strategy in Siu Nim Tau: to discover, without any threats, how to be comfortable while moving.

Your body weight is your power—if you move with the whole body at speed you optimize your force (f=ma) and you can also retreat or move around comfortably without getting hit.

Figure 10-30

Figure 10-31

Figure 10-32

Figure 10-33

Figure 10-34

Visual Cues: The Kicks within Siu Nim Tau

In the beginning the master needs to help his student make detailed adjustments, and the student needs to "supervise" his body. In the end the mind no longer needs to think; the body responds with the correct alignment intuitively.

The knee needs to be going forward in a straight line with the shin—if it is going backward it cannot kick and is liable to being kicked (which means it can be broken). In Figures 10-35 and 10-36, Sifu shows how Nick's toe pointing forward is exposing Nick's shin. If we kick with the toe we risk breaking the toe and also risk exposing the shin to a kick. Nick needs to turn his toe inward (Figure 10-41) to protect his shin and to allow him to counter kick. Sifu asks: "Where have you seen this before?—in the opening sequence of Siu Nim Tau."

"The novice does not realize that there are kicks within Siu Tim Tau. The position of the toes in this way also protects the groin. So Siu Nim Tau also prepares the body to protect itself. Through these exercises we try to develop the musculature memory—we want the body to remember, which is why a good master will be correcting the body structure of a student all the time until the body and mind connect together seamlessly. The practitioner 'supervises' his own body to align correctly until a certain harmony is felt within Siu Nim Tau. When that happens the mind no longer needs to think, the body responds with the correct alignment intuitively and it 'feels right.'

"In Figure 10-38 we can see that Nick's foot can be immobilized. If he moves his body to rescue his foot, his foot can be easily broken. With the incorrect positioning of the toes a

Figure 10-35

Figure 10-36

novice exposes his lower body to the real possibility of injury. This is why such detailed adjustments are so critical in the early stages of practice."

Note that if Nick attempts to lift his back foot he will be off balance and fall down—Sifu has effectively immobilized both feet due to the incorrect positioning of Nick's foot.

Figure 10-37

Figure 10-38

Figure 10-39

Figure 10-40

Figure 10-41

Figure 10-42

If Sifu's stomping kick is forceful, Nick's toes can be broken. The only way to avoid injury with a stomping kick would be if Nick was wearing strong tactical boots or reinforced work boots. When Sifu has instructed military or special forces in the past he has pointed out that even if the opponent's toes cannot be broken (in case they are wearing tactical footwear) the stomp kick will still immobilize their lower body and set them up for a takedown or fall.

Figure 10-43

Figure 10-44

Figure 10-45

Figure 10-46

Figure 10-47

After Sifu's adjustments Nick demonstrates the kick attacking the knees, shins, and toes (Figures 10-44 through 10-47).

Visual Cues: Wing Chun Fighting Stance

Figure 10-48

Figure 10-49

Figure 10-50

Sifu Loukas demonstrates the Wing Chun fighting stance. The body can comfortably move in response to whatever direction an attack comes from with economy of motion. This is the stance to begin with when expecting an attack. Do not confuse the Siu Nim Tau horse stance with a fighting stance. That stance is to train the correct body structure and shifting. It is not the stance to fight in. Do not fall foul of this misconception. As Sifu points out, "Be aware of Wing Chun's many optical illusions."

Visual Cues: Defense to a Grappling Attack

Figure 10-51

Figure 10-52

Wing Chun prepares you for any kind of street scenario. Sifu demonstrates a defense to a grappling attack.
Here Nick is attacking by forcefully grabbing Sifu. Loukas responds by using his elbows to create distance, forcing Nick to crash into the elbows. By simultaneously pivoting his body Sifu redirects the attack to the side, incorporating a throwing technique into the counter.

Figure 10-53

Figure 10-54

Figure 10-55

As Sifu says, "The opponent tells you how he would like to be hit."
By coming in with a grab and the intention to throw, Nick has caused injury to himself by crashing into Sifu's elbows and ends up being thrown to the ground.

Figure 10-56

Figure 10-57

Figure 10-58

Visual Cues: Arm Locks within Siu Nim Tau

Figure 10-59

"All the advanced forms lead you back to Siu Nim Tau."

Arm locks are also used in Wing Chun. These can be seen in the second part of Siu Nim Tau although they are not often recognized. Notice that in the second part of Siu Nim Tau we use two hands— to train the body to execute and to avoid arm locks (among other things). The second part of Siu Nim Tau has techniques of arm locks, grappling and take downs—all aspects examined and trained further in *chum-kiu*. The third part of Siu Nim Tau contains *biu-jee* techniques. This is why Sifu Loukas says that "all of the advanced forms lead you back to Siu Nim Tau."

During chi sao practice it is good to involve armlock techniques because a complete fighter should be able to blend all ranges of fighting—striking, grappling, kicks, takedowns, and locks. Wing Chun training should prepare you for all aspects of life-threatening situations.

Figure 10-60

Figure 10-61

Figure 10-62

Figure 10-63

In Figures 10-63 through 10-67 Nick has executed an armlock. Sifu Loukas counterattacks by extending his arm, shifting his body, and trapping Nick's hand. This creates an opening for an arm bar and elbow strike (potentially breaking the opponent's arm). Finally Sifu only has to move back with his entire body structure, resulting in a clean sweep that sends Nick to the floor and ends the

Figure 10-64

Figure 10-65

fight. Notice how if executed with full force Nick's head would crash into the ground in a potentially devastating injury. Good Wing Chun sets up the opponent using the environment and context to finish the fight efficiently with the minimum of fuss.

Figure 10-66

Figure 10-67

*

THE FIVE ELEMENTS

In oriental philosophy and martial arts, teachers often refer to the five elements as a pedagogical tool for helping their students understand the deeper principles of their art. The five elements refer to Earth, Wind, Water, Fire, and Void. It is fitting that one of the earliest historical figures to write about these elements was actually a Greek philosopher by the name of Empedocles. Being Greek himself, Loukas has adapted the five-element model to explain Wing Chun in his own terms, mixing oriental philosophy with his own experience and observations. In Loukas's model the "Ground" or "Earth" represents *strength* and *stability*; "Wind" is for *lightness, speed, fast actions,* and *forward energy*; "Water" represents *fluidity, power* (when packed together), and the ability to *effortlessly change shape*; and Fire is *hot, panicking, burning,* and *stinging*. The *Void* represents "no-technique as technique."

"There are priorities in the system," explains Loukas. "First, recover the central line (Earth); second, don't be in front of the attack—shifting like the Wind, trap hands or legs or both (Water); destroy body structure simultaneously in order to strike (Fire); and then last of all the techniques of Wing Chun come in. So the techniques such as lap-sau, pak-sau and so forth are last, not first. This is the meaning of *no technique as technique*. This is the way Wing Chun strategies and skills come to life.

The "Nim" in Siu Nim Tau means "theory," "philosophy," "program," "idea." Theory without practice does not work (and vice versa). Combat needs the second form as well (*Chum Kiu*). If you have the first and second forms, including the wooden dummy techniques, then your fighting skills are complete—but you haven't learned the full system. Theory needs to be backed with practical action. In the school we are training for fighting. Training for fighting and fighting itself are very different. If you have fighting in mind in the school, you will be under the illusion that your partner is your real opponent. You will not be able to use that training to fight in the streets. In the school you are *training* for fighting, in the streets you *are* fighting. If you are fighting with rules (such as in competition) you need to know the rules well in order to break the rules in real life. What works in the ring may not work in the streets (and vice versa). The way you are training and the way you need to fight are two different things. Enjoy the growth process but in a real-life fight don't think about technique, don't think about tan-sau or bong-sau. Think about hitting and not getting hit. This is why Wing Chun is a system not a style. All good fighters move in similar ways. The best fighters work with optimal biomechanics and efficiency. The joy of Wing Chun is to train hard and enjoy the process of personal growth and development. Do not think about fighting. But by practicing Wing Chun and internalizing its principles you will be ready for any kind of fight life brings you.

PART FOUR
STRATEGIES FOR LIFE

"The best soldier is not soldierly;
The best fighter is not ferocious;
The best conqueror does not take part in war;..."

—*Lao Tzu*[27]

In this concluding part of the book, we invite you to go beyond the technical details of Wing Chun and consider the implications of its principles for succeeding in all aspects of life—not just in physical fighting.

With examples taken from many different areas of life, Munawar draws out some of the most useful lessons that Wing Chun can teach us about how to approach real-world challenges outside of the training hall.

After reading this section we invite you to revisit the lives of the Wing Chun masters detailed in the first part of this book, and also to reflect on how Wing Chun can help you deal with current and future challenges in your own life.

---

27. Lao Tzu, *Tao Te Ching*, Ch'u Ta-Kao (trans.), George Allen & Unwin Ltd, 1937

11

BEYOND FIGHTING

What Wing Chun Can Teach Us About Life

MUNAWAR ALI KARIM

*"The true value of sword-fencing cannot be seen within
the confines of sword-fencing technique."*

—*Musashi Miyamoto (A Book of Five Rings)*

We began this book with stories of some of the great Wing Chun masters of the past. Just as they were instrumental in the development and transmission of Wing Chun into modern times, there is no doubt that Wing Chun itself was an important factor in how they dealt with the very real challenges of their own lives in their own times. From opposing foreign occupation, surviving against the backdrop of the Second World War and the communist revolution, to rising above gang-culture, tackling racist stereotypes and introducing a new cinematic art form to the world, each of them seems to have applied the principles and strategies of Wing Chun to achieve success outside of the training hall and the battlefield. For some, like Bruce Lee, the achievements have been dramatic, impacting in some way the entire world. For others the success has, perhaps, been more personal. What is clear however is that Wing Chun, when understood deeply, has the potential to not only train us in how to deal with the realities of physical combat but also to teach us how to deal with the complexities of our everyday lives. As we come to the end of this book we would like to leave you with some clues about how Wing Chun can provide you with not only skills for combat but also strategies for life.

As we have seen, the effectiveness of Wing Chun rests on the fact that it is driven by principles rather than being a selection of choreographed techniques. As a practitioner develops in his ability to instinctively move according to these principles in a combat situation, he experiences the truth of those principles. If, as you practice Wing Chun, you can take the feeling of that experience and translate it to other aspects of your life, you will come to realize the deeper aspects of an art that enhances the quality of everything you choose to do. Take another look at the lives of some of the great masters of Wing Chun whose histories we briefly explored in the first part of this book, and you will find that Wing Chun remained a guiding force for all of them their whole life long. In what follows we will attempt to briefly explore key aspects of Wing Chun principles, strategy, and tactics in the context of life outside of physical combat. In doing this we will draw on a wide range of examples as clues to help elucidate what we are saying and to help you explore these ideas through your own practice.

Each of our lives is unique and the myriad ways of the world are vast and complicated. And yet there are also patterns in the world that we are able to discern and understand. By exploring and reflecting on these patterns we can manipulate the world around us through technology, through scientific discoveries, through labeling and categorizing things, in order to fulfill our needs. When we do this in a positive way we can produce a great deal of good in the world—for example, advances in medicine. When we fall into negativity we end up producing a great deal of destruction in the world—such as the advances in military technology that enable us to cause destruction in ever more sophisticated ways and even to wipe out the entire human race through nuclear weapons. Or think of the unrestrained exploitation of the earth's resources that threatens to destroy the delicate balance of the eco-system and lead us to extinction. It would be impossible in a single chapter, or even in a single book, to explore in minute detail all of these complexities of human existence on a personal and global level with regards to the physical, intellectual, and spiritual aspects of a human being. What is possible however is to draw out universal principles—which can be seen in many places in different ways. Those principles are there to be discovered in Wing Chun as they are in other arts—in floral arrangement, painting, music, poetry, geometry, and calligraphy. In some arts they are easier to discern than in others. And in some contexts they will certainly lead you towards destruction.

In what follows I tentatively draw out some of these principles with examples from different contexts of life to show how we can see them being implemented. The examples come from all kinds of areas of life, from non-martial artists who achieved extraordinary results as well as from leaders of movements and empires. We are not saying that Wing Chun is the solution to life's problems. It is not a religion or an ideology, neither is it revelation. What we are saying is that Wing Chun practice can teach you how to successfully negotiate life's challenges because as you practice it you can begin to see—if you look out for it—rules of engagement that work in a fight as they do in other aspects of life. I hope that the reader will reflect on this chapter in the context of all that we have said before—particularly in the context of the lives of the Wing Chun masters of the past and through the practice of Wing Chun discover what works to improve all aspects of their life and the lives of others.

The First Principle: STRUCTURE

*To be successful in your objective you must first build and
then maintain a structure that enables you to achieve it.*

The Basic Idea:
1. The entire structure should be optimized to achieve the purpose or "end in mind."
2. First you have to be absolutely clear on your purpose.
3. Second you have to set up a structure that is completely invested in achieving this purpose with maximum efficiency.

Up Close:
   A Wing Chun practitioner has one goal in mind when he or she is engaged in a physical conflict: to end the fight by disabling the opponent's ability to pose a threat. Wing Chun approaches this by directing its entire system to overcome the opponent's centerline. In a sense, controlling, capturing, or subduing the opponent's centerline is what the entire system is focused on. For Wing Chun the path to victory is clear—it lies at the end of (or *through*) the centerline. Capture that and you have won because your opponent will no longer be able to offer you any threat.
   As we have seen in the previous chapters of this book, Wing Chun achieves this objective by emphasizing "structure"—everything from the way the Wing Chun practitioner places his or her feet, to how he aligns his body in terms of the relationship between his hands, elbows, shoulders, hips, knees, ankles, and his own centerline are a part of this structure. This means a Wing Chun practitioner, when he is doing Wing Chun in a fight, has set up his entire body with one single-minded objective that is designed to achieve the ultimate strategic victory as understood by Wing Chun. If he is spectacularly successful in achieving this objective the fight should be over within one or two moves. This is because the structure enables the strategic objective to be obtained with maximum efficiency. Every part of the Wing Chun practitioner's body and mind has been recruited to work toward this ultimate goal—nothing has been wasted. No part of his body has been left without purpose—for example, both hands are active when punching. And both hands are working toward the same purpose. Usually the opponent is not thinking like this. Typically the threat—the attacker or aggressor—is directing his force to hit you or hurt you as much as possible with little structural alignment toward the end goal. Partly this is because they have not even clarified the end goal. That is to say, they have not defined what "victory" means. In previous parts of this book we have described this as a scenario where two opponents are exchanging blows—like in a boxing match. This is brutal, ugly, and terribly destructive. It is not Wing Chun.

The greatest and most effective masters of their disciplines intuitively understand and practice this principle. Musashi Miyamoto, the great Japanese samurai "sword-saint" and strategist, described his way of swordsmanship unequivocally with the following words: "In short, the way of the Ichi school is the spirit of winning, whatever the weapon and whatever its size."[28] And he then goes on to explain how other sword schools have lost sight of this important objective and gone astray: "As if with the nut and the flower, the nut has become less than the flower."[29] Whereas other schools taught swordsmanship with the use of the sword in one hand, Musashi Miyamoto, describing his path as the path of "Two Heavens, One Way," uniquely emphasizes the use of two swords—one in each hand. His "one way" is the way of cutting—killing the opponent in mortal combat. When the stakes are so high, why would you neglect to make use of both your hands?

In this example, we can see that Musashi clearly understood his purpose: to cut down the opponent. And he then recruits all of his tools to achieve that purpose. He explains this concept in detail in the first part of his *A Book of Five Rings*, comparing his "Way of Strategy" to the "Way of the Carpenter."

Business guru Stephen Covey discovered this same principle when he examined the lives of what he described as "the most highly effective people" in history.[30] They all begin with an end in mind. He made this idea the second habit in what he regarded as the seven habits of highly effective people throughout human history: "Begin with the end in mind."[31]

When a Wing Chun practitioner successfully maintains his structure in chi-sau practice, he finds he is more easily able to engage his limbs correctly in response to his partner's actions, and his body responds as if completely without effort to attack and destabilize his opponent's centerline. If his opponent is not as competent as him, the opponent cannot respond—the flow of the practice is often disrupted. The game is effectively over because the more competent practitioner has achieved his objective and won as a result of superior adherence to the structure and body mechanics of Wing Chun. And so repeated exposure to this practice drives home the reality that maintaining one's Wing Chun structure—the principles of which are taught and refined in the forms, and in chi-sau—is the quickest, and most painless path to victory.

And so it is in life. First clarify the end in mind. And then invest the time, energy, and practice in building a structure that will allow you to achieve this objective with as much efficiency and grace as possible. Let us take some actual examples of this principle at play in different areas of real life.

---

28. Viktor Harris, tr., *A Book of Five Rings* (Woodstock, NY: Flamingo, 1984), 35.
29. *A Book of Five Rings*, 28.
30. Stephen, R. Covey, *The Seven Habits of Highly Effective People* (New York: Simon & Schuster, 1989).
31. Ibid., *94*.

Case Study: Dr. Maria Montessori and the Classroom
Maria Montessori was the first female physician in Italy. In 1890, when she was twenty years old and had just finished graduate school, she decided she wanted to become a doctor. At that time in Italy it was unheard of for women to pursue a medical career and she had to overcome many obstacles to get admitted into medical school to pursue her interests. When it was clear that she was not going to gain admission as "Maria" Montessori, she gave her name on the application form as "Mario" Montessori. "The administrators (and professors) assuming that the candidate was a male, and being impressed with "Mario's" academic credentials, accepted the application. We can only imagine the shock and embarrassment on their faces when they realized that they had been outsmarted by this clever young lady. After all there was no difference between "Mario" and "Maria" except for a single letter of the alphabet! They were left with no choice but to let her join the all-male cohort of students.

Montessori's greatest legacy to the world however was not in medicine but in education. She went on to found a method of teaching that to this very day—more than a hundred years later—benefits children from all around the world. Jeff Bezos, founder of Amazon, Larry Page and Sergey Brin, founders of Google, Wikipedia founder Jimmy Wales, and a host of other influential people in modern times all benefitted from a Montessori education. Many of them attribute their success to their early school experience as Montessori students.

One of the unique aspects of Montessori education is the structured environment. Children are free to choose whatever activities they wish to do within the classroom. However, every aspect of the classroom itself is designed with one single objective in mind—to enable the child to learn through self-exploration as much as possible those skills which are developmentally suited to the child within a certain age range. These classrooms or "Children's Houses" usually have natural wooden furniture, no teacher's desk, no "lecturing" from the blackboard. Instead, carefully designed "Montessori materials" are beautifully arranged on low shelves easily accessible by children who are free to take these materials and "play" with them for as long and as often as they like until they achieve the specific learning outcomes the materials are designed to help them discover. The teacher is a guide, not an instructor—he or she will model for the child how to handle and use the material and introduce more complexity into the environment as and when needed. Children move around freely, select work of their own accord, discover what for them are "new insights" about the world—for example, the relationship between the symbol "3" and a quantity of three objects, or how long-division works, or how to identify the subject and object of a sentence. Or even how to lay a table and fold a napkin. They will choose for themselves when they wish to have a snack during their "work" and generally move around in the classroom in a way which seems extraordinary and unbelievable for adults used to only seeing conventional schooling models. When visitors see children in a Montessori "classroom" it seems to them as if they are observing little adults at work. Even more extraordinary for the visitors is that these children are able to "work" like this uninterrupted for almost three hours without at all feeling bored or becoming distracted. Instead, they take a short snack break at a designated "snack table" (which normally contains a vase of flowers) at a time of their own choosing and come back to their work with no insistence from the teacher.

All this is possible for one main reason: the classroom has been designed with a singular objective in mind. Just as Wing Chun teaches the practitioner to maintain a structure that enables him to protect his centerline and dominate the opponent's centerline, Montessori teachers maintain within their classrooms what they call the "prepared environment" where everything is designed to help the child focus on and learn those things which are developmentally appropriate for his or her age range. In fact not only the classroom, but also the materials that are placed within it, how they are arranged, the type of furniture, the layout and design, the displays on the wall, the arrangement of decorations, the proximity to the outdoors, the tone of voice of the teacher, and how he or she moves around the environment—every single aspect has been structured to enable the child to achieve the objective. This is a clear and quite charming example of the importance of two things: 1. Clarifying the end in mind. 2. Designing and maintaining a structure that enables one to realize that objective. In the Montessori classroom we can see what the Wing Chung practitioner experiences in the kwoon—a structure that is completely aligned with the end in mind. The Wing Chun practitioner can see this fundamental principle at work in his practice of combat when he is able to effortlessly overcome an aggressive opponent. Over time he releases the importance of structure to enable correct body mechanics and end the fight. In the Montessori classroom the structure is designed to enable independent learning in an atmosphere of self-discovery that naturally aligns with children's inherent curiosity and playfulness. Why was 'independent' learning important to Maria Montessori? Probably because she realized from her own life's experiences battling sexism in a European society that tried to deny her the pursuit of her medical studies (and later confronting the specter of fascism under Mussolini), that the most important thing in education was to teach young people how to learn and think for themselves. In a very real sense, what one woman—Ng Mei—understood in the domain of combat, another woman—Maria Montessori—understood in the field of education: to be successful in our objective we must first build and then maintain a structure that enables us to achieve it.

The Montessori-educated founders of the biggest tech giants of our time have also understood this principle. And with it they have, whether we like it or not, built such powerful "eco-systems" that we have all been forced to (re)structure our lives in accordance with their businesses. In Wing Chun terms we might say that they have captured and dominated our "centerlines" and maybe even set the entire world off-balance.

Case Study: Structure and MacDonald's
MacDonald's is another good example of the overwhelming power of having a clear objective in mind and aligning the entire structure of an organization to meet that objective. Whatever we may think of the company's morals and the quality of its food, there is little doubt that as a business it is one of the most successful in modern times. If you go into a

MacDonald's restaurant anywhere in the world, you can expect almost exactly the same food delivered in almost exactly the same time in almost exactly the same way. This ruthlessly meticulous consistency is possible because MacDonald's has refined every aspect of what food is prepared, how it is prepared, and how it is sold. Everything from the temperature of the ovens to the time taken to receive and process an order has been carefully analyzed, optimized, and systematized. Because the structure is so tightly aligned with its profit-making strategy it is able to replicate its business almost anywhere in the world and give its customers the same experience regardless of where they are on the planet. This has meant that MacDonald's has been able to grow into one of the largest franchise businesses on the globe and also one of the largest real estate businesses. Its structure is always aligned to produce maximum efficiency in making a profit for its owners.

Action Points
1. Spend time clarifying what you want to achieve (define what success means to you).
2. Then spend time clarifying the optimal strategy to realize that end.
3. Then design and build your entire structure to achieve that end in mind in the most efficient way possible.

The Second Principle: THE OBSTACLE SHOWS THE WAY

Follow the path of least resistance

The Basic Idea:
1. Do not meet force with force, resistance with resistance.
2. Stay calm and relaxed as much as possible so that you can sense (or be mindful of) where and what the insurmountable obstacles are. This will help you locate the empty spaces.
3. Head in the direction of the 'emptiness' to find your path to success

Up Close:
   As we learned in the first part of this book, Wing Chun masters take pride in tracing the origins of their fighting art to a woman—Ng Mei. The origin story of Wing Chun teaches us that this is a method of fighting which is intelligent—it does not pitch brute force against brute force. Rather it uses the skillful application of body mechanics and leverage to overcome aggression and subdue an opponent. It is a way of 'fighting without fighting.' We have seen this clearly outlined in a practical way in the second part of this book where we have explored actual Wing Chun training, techniques, and drills. And we have seen how in chi-

sau practice the emphasis is on being relaxed while under pressure. As a person's Wing Chun improves, he discovers that only when he is relaxed, only when he finds his way around the obstacle, only when he chooses to head in the direction of the empty space and not against the force opposing him, can he move forward and obtain victory in an almost effortless way. And so it is with all aspects of our life. This is what Bruce Lee had in mind when he made his now famous comments about being like water on the *Pierre Berton Show* (quoted earlier in this book):

> *Empty your mind, be formless, shapeless, like water. Now you put water into a cup, it becomes the cup. You put water into a bottle, it becomes the bottle. You put it in a teapot, it becomes the teapot. Now water can flow, or it can crash! Be water, my friend.*

Case Study: Bruce Lee and Ip Man

We can see many instances of Bruce Lee making use of this principle in his own life. We have already seen in Chapter 3 how Lee tackled rumors circulating in the Hong Kong press about his criticism of Wing Chun. Newspaper articles at that time were deliberately provocative, using Bruce Lee's outspoken criticism of traditional Kung-fu practice as a means to stir controversy in the Wing Chun and wider Hong Kong martial arts community. Grandmaster Ip Man was also unhappy with these reports and how they were stirring up hatred within his Wing Chun fraternity. Initially, Lee tried to tackle the exaggerated newspaper reporting head-on but that only made things worse as Matthew Polly explains in his biography of Lee:

> *The China Star, a Hong Kong tabloid, ran a multipart series supposedly written by Ip Chun, the son of Ip Man, about what Bruce was like as a teenage Kung-fu student. In the fourth part, Ip Chun wrote that he had seen the young Bruce Lee get knocked down by an opponent during training due to a flaw in his technique. The flaw in the story was Ip Chun never trained with Bruce when they were teenagers. He didn't arrive in Hong Kong until 1965, long after Bruce had moved to America. Taking this article as a public insult, Bruce angrily confronted Ip Chun to ask if he had really said what had been printed. Ip Chun denied everything, blaming the reporter who had ghostwritten the article in his name. Bruce tracked down and accosted the reporter. As Hong Kong's first genuine superstar, Bruce was the bread and butter of tabloids like The China Star. Its owner and editor, Graham Jenkins, a hardbitten Australian newspaperman of the Rupert Murdoch mold, published a follow-up story, filled with mock outrage, saying that Bruce had threatened the paper's informant and had forced him to change his story. Now they had managed to make Bruce look like a punk and a bully. Further enraged, Bruce sued The China Star for libel. "His logic was if you don't draw the line, it's just going to go on and on," says Andre Morgan. But it did go on and on. Having baited the bull, every thrash of his horns was fresh copy. The China Star gleefully wrote about the lawsuit.*

> *As the controversy grew, other newspapers began reporting that Bruce had disrespected his master, Ip Man, and Ip Man was angry at Lee, quoting Wing Chun students who were avenging Bruce's slights.*
>
> *In traditional Confucian culture, children, students, and disciples were supposed to be deferential and devoted to their parents, teachers, and masters. The Cultural Revolution in mainland China (1966–76) was upending that power relationship with children turning on their parents, students on their teachers, and disciples on their masters. Its reverberations were being felt in Hong Kong, terrifying the authorities. By espousing individual freedom and a rejection of tradition, Bruce had aligned himself philosophically with the youth revolt. Rumors of a troubled relationship with Ip Man became a kind of shorthand for these larger societal rifts. Conservative outlets, who lionized Bruce as a Chinese hero after the patriotic Fist of Fury, were now painting him as too Western, too modern, not Chinese enough.[32]*

It is telling that for his part Ip Man, unlike Lee, did not even try to tackle the rumors head on. Instead, both men simply put an end to the gossip by going out for afternoon tea and taking a long walk along the busy Nathan Road so that everyone could see them genuinely enjoying each other's company. The whole episode is such a wonderful illustration of this principle in practice that it is worth requoting the passage already cited in Chapter 3:

> *The truth was Bruce respected Ip Man, and Ip Man liked Up-start. Whatever larger critique he was making in public, Bruce was extremely polite and solicitous to Ip Man in person. Whatever reservations Ip Man may have felt about Bruce's public remarks about traditional Kung-fu, he was clever enough to appreciate that having the most famous martial arts actor in Asia as one of his disciples was a net positive for him. To quash rumors of a rift, Bruce invited Ip Man out for yum cha (afternoon tea and dim sum) at a restaurant near Kowloon Park. While they ate, Bruce smiled at Ip Man and asked, "Do you still treat me as your student?"*
>
> *Ip Man quickly replied, "Do you still treat me as your sifu?" Both men laughed.*
>
> *After they were done, Bruce said, "Sifu, we haven't gone for a walk together in a long time. How about we take a walk?" They strolled along the very busy Nathan Road so the public could see that their relationship was good."[33]*

In this exchange of a master and a student—who was now forging a new path for himself—the most telling aspect is the exchange of questions between Sifu Ip Man and Bruce Lee: "Do you still treat me as your student?" says Lee. "Do you still treat me as your sifu?" replies Ip Man. They both laugh. And then Lee immediately addresses his old master as sifu. In this exchange, as in the whole episode, we can see Wing Chun being expressed in the

---

32. Polly (2018, Ibid). 531
33. Ibid. 532

context of real life—a simple principle of not tackling force with force, but rather letting the obstacle show us the way, and following the path of least resistance to quash the potentially reputation-destroying gossip machine of the tabloid press.

Case Study—the Great Plains Bison and the American Railroads

When track was being laid for railroads in North America, surveyors found that the best routes had already been suggested for them. For centuries, herds of Great Plains bison had been following what the musician and management consultant Robert Fritz calls "the path of least resistance":

> *As they moved through the land, they placed one foot in front of the next. Each step guided the next step. What determined each step was the topography—the contour of the earth. When faced with a sudden incline, a group of rocks, or a thorny stubble, the bison would adjust their course and seek the easiest next step.*
>
> *Step led to step and way led to way, deepening the path over time. Each new herd that travelled through the land found it natural to move where their predecessors had gone before.*
>
> *The bison were following the laws of nature [...] And in nature, energy moves where it is easiest to go. This is the principle of the path of least resistance.*[34]

Case Study—The Conquest of Constantinople

To make use of this principle you have to be completely convinced that the obstacle can truly show you the way. In other words, you have to change your perspective on how you think about the obstacle or challenge that seems to be preventing you from obtaining your objective. A mountain or a wall in front of you is not stopping you from obtaining your objective, rather it is signposting you to go left or right.

In 1453 the Ottoman leader—Sultan Mehmed II—besieged the mighty Byzantine city of Constantinople. The city was well defended due to its geography and its massive walled fortifications. The walls were well-nigh impossible to breach by force and the only access by sea was through the Golden Horn—a stretch of water linking the city to the Bosporus. The Byzantines controlled access to the Golden Horn by the use of a massive chain they had erected across the water. They would lower the chain in order to receive fresh supplies from Venetian ships and raise it again when Ottoman ships approached. The walled fortifications were an impregnable obstacle by land preventing access to the city, and the chain was an impregnable obstacle by sea preventing a proper blockade and making the land-siege futile. The last bastion of the Roman Empire, Constantinople had for

---

34. Robert Fritz, *The Path of Least Resistance for Managers* (San Francisco: Berrett-Koehler Publishers, 1999), 1.

centuries been considered an unconquerable city. In a stunning example of ingenuity Sultan Mehmed understood what these obstacles were telling him. He realized the futility of trying to constantly attack these positions head on and understood that the obstacles were showing him the proper direction to send his navy—not over the sea but over land, not through the chain, but around it.

With stunning ingenuity and determination the Ottomans literally hauled their navy over land using a conveyor belt of hastily constructed logs. Sometimes uphill and often across difficult terrain they managed to transport their ships over land, avoiding the chain defenses altogether. The fleet was gently rolled back into the sea on the other side of the chain all in the space of one night. At the break of dawn the Byzantines awoke to discover the Ottoman fleet inside the Golden Horn while the chain remained in place. The presence of the Ottoman fleet on the inside of the chain now made it impossible for Venetian ships to send supplies. Shortly after this tactical shift a victorious Ottoman army would march into Constantinople and the Sultan would be declared the new emperor of Rome. Since we are talking about perspective, this last point is important. The Ottomans never considered themselves outsiders—but rather rightful heirs to Roman glory under a new pax-Ottomana. They would go on to revive and expand the glory of the city and make it the magical place it remains to this day.

Case Study—Rosa Park's Bus Boycott

As late as 1955 African-Americans were still suffering under Segregation in the southern states of the US. Among the many injustices was the expectation in Alabama that black people should give up their seats for white people on buses. When an African-American lady, Rosa Parks, refused to give up her seat for a white man she was arrested and taken to court.

Black leaders and activists realized that the only way they would be allowed equal rights when riding the buses in Alabama was to stop riding the buses. Over a series of meetings and discussions the African-American community decided on a course of action that may well have seemed counterintuitive at the time but which history now recalls as one of the key moments in the ongoing struggle for civil rights in America. The boycott lasted 381 days and ultimately helped propel the Reverend Martin Luther King to prominence as a civil rights leader. Although they may not have articulated it in this way at the time, the black men and women in Alabama had used the very obstacle of repression to show them how to break through its tyranny—not by forcibly sitting on the buses, but by giving them up altogether.

Action Points
1. Understand that the obstacle or challenge that seems insurmountable is there to show you how to reach your objective. This requires a change of perspective on your part.
2. Instead of trying to force your way through it, try to understand how it can direct you towards success.

3. Follow the path of least resistance to discover the solution. When you find that path, be daring enough to take it. The path of least resistance may not be easy—it takes effort to haul ships over dry-land, or to boycott public transport and walk miles to work a long shift and then take the long walk home again. But the way that the obstacle is showing you, is indeed the way. Be brave enough to take that road.

The Third Principle: KEEP MOVING FORWARD

Do not fear moving forward slowly, fear only to stand still

The Basic Idea:
1. At no moment should you be standing still—at each instant you should be moving closer to your objective, even if it is slowly.
2. Every action you undertake should be bringing you closer to achieving your goal.
3. To achieve this, you must have the previous two principles in place.

Up Close:
In previous chapters of this book we have talked about the importance of what Sifu Loukas calls "forward spring-loaded energy." A Wing Chun practitioner's energy is always moving forward in the direction of the opponents centerline. Like a river surging down a mountain, following the landscape's twists and turns but always heading toward the sea, the Wing Chun practitioner has a kind of momentum that keeps him or her constantly applying a kind of forward "pressure." This is seen in its most basic form in the Wing Chun chain punching and felt in its most sophisticated expression in the practice of chi-sau. It is important to understand that this forward energy is not a forceful crashing into the opponent's defenses but rather seeking the path of least resistance to obtain the goal with a minimum of effort. When chi-sau becomes effortless and the two practitioners seem to flow in an unending, seamless exchange of movement, it means that they both have good structure and an appropriate level of relaxation. The structure enables the forward spring-loaded energy, the relaxation ensures that you can sense what the obstacle is telling you—you can feel and follow the path of least resistance. Having now said this, it should be clear that this principle requires that the previous two principles be properly internalized. In life, as in Wing Chun, your "structure" should encourage forward moving energy and the ability to sense the obstacles so that you can naturally respond and adapt to the changing landscape of your life's journey while still heading towards your goal.

It also means that once you have embarked on a course of action you do not abruptly stop but are resolved to keep the momentum of your actions going until the desired objective is achieved. In Wing Chun—as we have seen—the objective is not to exchange blows, and so a Wing Chun practitioner does not launch a single punch and then bob and weave waiting for a response as if in a sparring match but rather moves in a rapid flow of motion directed by structure, body mechanics, and sensitivity to the obstacle until he has ended the fight.

Case Study—Learning How to Drive or Play the Piano

For this principle a simple example should suffice. Let's say you wish to learn how to drive a car or play the piano. Taking three lessons every week for a month with a good instructor is a great plan. But if you take three lessons a week this month but then the following month decide to skip a few lessons and only end up taking three lessons for the whole of that month, you are losing "forward moving energy." Perhaps your enthusiasm is waning because you realize that driving (or playing the piano) is harder than you thought. It doesn't seem fun anymore. Or you "don't feel too well," you really don't want to miss that party this week, or for some other reason. If you do not maintain a consistent "forward" motion you will make it much more difficult for you to master your goal and may never get your driver's license or learn to play the piano. It may even be that you cannot take regular lessons because you can't afford to—that of course may seem like a legitimate excuse. Actually what this means is that you haven't thought about "structure" carefully (the first principle). A better approach—the "Wing Chun" approach if you like—would be to first save enough funds in a separate bank account so that when you begin your lessons your "structure" enables you to easily continue taking regular instruction until you are ready to go for that final test. Alternatively, you could take fewer lessons every week but take them regularly. It may take longer to reach your goal but remember: *do not fear moving forward slowly, fear only to stand still*. If you are not consistent you may as well be standing still.

Another typical reason for losing forward momentum with our big goals is the feeling that we keep getting interrupted, or that we just "don't have enough time." Again this comes down to structure—everyone has time to brush their teeth and take a bath. Why is that? Because everyone knows the consequences of not doing so. In other words you know that you have to make time for these things because it would be unbearable not to. In the same way, if the objective is truly so important to you then you have to make time for it. So structure that time into your calendar as an appointment that you can never allow yourself to miss. Structure all your other commitments around that goal if you have to, but don't ever let anything get in the way of the time allocated to the purpose that is so important to you.

Everyone who has mastered any art, skill, or discipline has done so through the consistent practice of that discipline.

Action Points
1. Make sure Principle 1 (STRUCTURE) is not only clearly designed to help you achieve your goal but is also designed to ensure that you do not stop or waiver until you have accomplished it.
2. Once you set out on your course of action—the business plan, the piano lessons, the school studies, the MBA or even raising your kids—be resolved to work consistently at it and do not allow anything to get in the way of the time and resources you have allocated to that noble project.
3. If you do run into obstacles that seem insurmountable remember Principle 2: THE OBSTACLE SHOWS THE WAY.

The Fourth Principle: TIMING

Winning does not mean being first (sometimes being on time means being late).

The Basic Idea:
1. Don't rush foolishly into things because other people are doing the same thing.
2. Take time to understand your context—the terrain, the marketplace, the employer.
3. Let others go first if they want to. They can help build the bridges for you to cross.
4. Often winning means being last not being first.

Up Close:
　In previous chapters we have seen that when your opponent strikes first they often show you how they can be hit. In a sense they put out a "bridge" which you can easily follow allowing you a clear path into their centerline and a way to trap and immobilize their threat. In our times people are always keen to be first as if this is a guarantee of success. Even in a race where the actual objective is to be first past the finish line it doesn't necessarily mean you must or should be the first to leave the start line. For example, in an endurance race those who pace themselves and know when to rest or slow down and when to press on and speed up are often the ones who arrive at the finish line on time—in other words, first. They do not think of starting "first," they simply start 'on time' and set the pace that optimizes their chance of success.

Case Study—Netflix and the Last Blockbuster

Beginning in 1984, Blockbuster offered movie and video game rentals through their chains of stores in the US. As the business grew Blockbuster stores expanded worldwide, making it a global operation. By contrast, Netflix was a latecomer to the movie rental business, being founded in 1997. Initially, Netflix followed Blockbuster's business model with similar rental fees and borrowing periods but with one crucial exception—Netflix offered its services online. Eventually Netflix dropped rental fees in favor of a subscription-based model offering customers unlimited streaming of movies for a regular monthly payment. Starting off with just thirty employees and ninety-two titles available, and at one point facing a possible acquisition from Blockbuster, Netflix is now considered one of the most successful online businesses to date while, at the time of writing, it appears that there is just one Blockbuster store left in the world (in Bend, Oregon, USA).[35] We needn't feel too sorry for the owners of the sole Blockbuster in the world, however. The store stocks around two thousand titles and has become somewhat of a tourist destination, known affectionately as "The Last Blockbuster." It is even the subject of a 2020 documentary by the same name.[36]

What does Netflix's relatively late entry into the movie rental business and Blockbuster's demise tell us? *You don't have to be first to win.* In a very real sense, however, the world's sole surviving Blockbuster says it even more clearly: *You don't have to be first, but you do have to be last.*

Action Points
1. Be very mindful of timing in all you do. Always factor timing into your strategy.
2. Ask yourself if being first is better than being last in your context? Does victory come from being late or being on time? For example, it might normally be good practice to arrive early or on time for meetings. It might sometimes be better to arrive late.
3. Don't let early success blind you to innovation and adaptation—remember that new challenges can show you the way too if you are still willing to learn from them.
4. Do not allow superficial deadlines to force you to make important decisions before you are ready. By the same token, do not put off important decisions or actions indefinitely. Free yourself from distracting influences and choose the timing that is best for your objective regardless of what others are doing.

---

35. Associated Press, "There's 1 Blockbuster Left in the US and Its Owner Refuses to Close," July 12th, 2018, https://nypost.com/2018/07/12/theres-1-blockbuster-left-in-the-us-and-its-owner-refuses-to-close/.
36. https://en.wikipedia.org/wiki/Blockbuster_(Bend,_Oregon).

Final Thoughts

The four principles outlined above are a brief insight into the fruits of my personal journey through Wing Chun. These ideas are not necessarily unique to Wing Chun and I have deliberately shared examples to illustrate them being used, consciously or otherwise, by people from different walks of life and historical periods. That this is the case—that Wing Chun embodies within it principles for combat that successful people implement in other areas of life—only enhances the value and specialness of Wing Chun. It means that to some extent Wing Chun is built upon universal truths.

In this albeit brief look at this hidden aspect of Wing Chun, I have tried to illustrate what I discovered early on in my Wing Chun practice and heard echoed by Sifu Loukas time and again in almost every training session: Wing Chun makes you better at everything you do. Wing Chun is a way that will not only teach you skills for combat but also strategies for life. And that for me is one of its great hidden treasures. By practicing Wing Chun with this mindset you will not only bring joy to your practice, but you will enrich it too. Moreover, you will find that Wing Chun, understood in this way, gives you a framework to improve all aspects of your life. Now that you have been shown something of this secret, I hope you will explore it further and make use of its treasures wisely.

AFTERWORD
Closing Thoughts On Wing Chun

SIFU LOUKAS KASTROUNIS

Wing Chun is to attain a high level of skill through hard work and practicing. There are no shortcuts, no easy ways to master the art, no easy ways to learn to defend yourself. You have to sweat for it and possibly end up with some bruises, cuts, definitely a bruised ego to be able to get your best from yourself and find your self-confidence. In fighting, there should be almost no indication that a fighter trains in Wing Chun because the movements and footwork should be as natural as possible. In truth, there are no styles in a fight. There are only good body mechanics and bad body mechanics. It should come as no surprise that all accomplished fighters move in similar ways.

In sports and competitions we have a winner and a runner-up, but in the old Olympics there was only one winner, no second best. Everyone was fighting to be the best. But nowadays in sports we have winners and runners-up. In jobs we have the best worker, worker of the year, and second best. But don't be deceived! In a street-fight there is only one winner. The second best will be injured or worse. Don't be satisfied with mediocrity. Try your best and train hard to bring out your best. In martial arts we train to be the best. We try to teach the brain how the system works and not to trust our eyes because the eyes can be fooled by optical illusions. As confidence develops around the system and with the training of the body it becomes practical and efficient.

Wing Chun is a sophisticated form of Kung-fu. Efficiency is going to be required for accuracy, and Wing Chun training helps develop that efficiency. It demands accuracy and simplicity, and this is not easy to attain until you develop your own confidence. But don't think of Wing Chun as simply another activity. To truly savor Wing Chun, it has to become a lifestyle, a life philosophy, a process of self-discovery, a process of quieting your mind, making your body into a weapon, and finding your fighting potential. Practicing Wing Chun makes everything else a little bit better. It's a subtle and deceptive art. It can benefit everyone but its true beauty is reserved for those open-minded, insightful, and discerning individuals worthy of its genius.

I reserve the right to be wrong. Re-examine what you find in these pages and see what works for you. Find your own truth and enjoy the journey!

About the Author

Munawar Ali Karim is a combatives instructor, natural movement coach, Montessori educator, and martial artist with an interest in history and sacred tradition. He is the author of *Liberty's Jihad: African Muslim Slaves and the Meaning of America,* a "compelling and illuminating ... work of historical criticism" (*Kirkus*). He holds undergraduate degrees in law and Japanese and a postgraduate degree in modern history. He began studying martial arts at the age of twelve with a Shotokan Karate master who also taught a hybrid style derived from Hung-Gar Kung-fu and Southern Praying Mantis (Chow-Gar). In his early twenties Munawar was invited to work for the Japanese government as an international relations specialist. Living in a small town in the Kiso Mountains along  the *nakasendo*—the old road between Edo and Tokyo—Munawar studied Shorinji Kempo whilst deepening his understanding of ninjutsu, samurai, and sufi teachings. On returning from Japan, Munawar continued to pursue the martial arts including Shaolin Kung Fu (under 33rd generation Shaolin Monk Shifu Zheng Ke Wang), Wing Chun (under Sifu Loukas Kastrounis) and Brazilian Jiu Jitsu (Gracie lineage).

In 2008 Munawar made the decision to leave his position as a corporate lawyer to pursue his interests in the development of mind, body, and spirit through teaching, writing, and personal practice. In 2009 he founded a not-for-profit Montessori Primary and Liberal Arts Secondary School to help young people of all backgrounds access an elite education rooted in traditional values. Aside from his formal practice of martial arts, Munawar enjoys epee fencing, poetry, and traditional archery. In 2019 he founded Deenway Dojo to share his interpretation of the martial way (*budo*) with others. Munawar describes his *budo* as following the maxim of the great "sword saint" Musashi Miyamoto: *bun bu ichi ryu* "Pen and Sword in Accord," and the spiritual teachings of the Sufi masters.

About the Author

Loukas Kastrounis is a third-generation direct descendant of Great Grand Master Ip Man through Sifu Wong Shun Leung. He completed the Wing Chun system with Master Nino Bernardo at the now legendary "Basement" school of Wing Chun in London. Master Wong was better known as Gong Sau Wong—*king of talking with the hands*—and was Bruce Lee's foremost Wing Chun teacher. Throughout the 1950s and 1960s Wong was undefeated in all of his challenges and recognised as one of Ip Man's best students and as the foremost instructor of the legendary martial artist and film star Bruce Lee. Master Nino Bernardo was one of the few who had completed the Wing Chun system in Hong Kong under Wong Shun Leung. Loukas was also taught Kali by Nino Bernado  (whose Kali lineage comes directly from world-famous Bruce Lee student and Kali master Guru Dan Inosanto). Loukas has been teaching Kali and Wing Chun to beginners and seasoned martial artists alike since 1992. Many advanced teachers and practitioners of Wing Chun, Karate, Taekwondo, Aikido, Kali, JKD, and boxing have taken instruction from Sifu Loukas. He has also provided specialist instruction to security firms, bodyguards, and law enforcement officers, including the military.

In 2000 he choreographed fighting scenes at the Sonning Mill Theatre in Berkshire (UK). In October 2003 Loukas was presented with the Hall of Fame Award by *Combat Magazine* at an award ceremony in Birmingham, UK, in recognition of his commitment to the development of Martial Arts in the United Kingdom and around the world. He has been featured in a number of martial arts magazines and newspaper articles in the UK and abroad and has been interviewed twice live on BBC Radio Berkshire. In September 2008 Loukas played a leading role in an action-combat martial arts film *Game Over*. This film was screened at various short film festivals around the world including the 2009 International Film Festival in Rome. The film won first position at the Tokyo Short film festival in Japan (2009), and second place in Hollywood, USA (2010).

In 2012 Loukas was interviewed by several Greek newspapers and the magazine *Rhodes Mirror*. In 2012 Kosmos TV broadcast an interview with Loukas discussing his Wing Chun teachings. This proved to be very popular, resulting in Kosmos TV broadcasting a half-hour documentary on Loukas's work in 2013. In 2014 the BBC aired a documentary focusing on Loukas's Wing Chun school in Reading, Berkshire. Loukas continues to teach Wing Chun in the UK and Europe, including to members of the armed forces. He is also founder of the European Wing Chun Association and travels frequently to teach and conduct seminars around the world.

BOOKS FROM YMAA

- 101 REFLECTIONS ON TAI CHI CHUAN
- 108 INSIGHTS INTO TAI CHI CHUAN
- A WOMAN'S QIGONG GUIDE
- ADVANCING IN TAE KWON DO
- ANALYSIS OF GENUINE KARATE
- ANALYSIS OF GENUINE KARATE 2
- ANALYSIS OF SHAOLIN CHIN NA 2ND ED
- ANCIENT CHINESE WEAPONS
- ART AND SCIENCE OF STAFF FIGHTING
- THE ART AND SCIENCE OF SELF-DEFENSE
- ART AND SCIENCE OF STICK FIGHTING
- ART OF HOJO UNDO
- ARTHRITIS RELIEF
- BACK PAIN RELIEF
- BAGUAZHANG
- BRAIN FITNESS
- CHIN NA IN GROUND FIGHTING
- CHINESE FAST WRESTLING
- CHINESE FITNESS
- CHINESE TUI NA MASSAGE
- COMPLETE MARTIAL ARTIST
- COMPREHENSIVE APPLICATIONS OF SHAOLIN CHIN NA
- CONFLICT COMMUNICATION
- DAO DE JING: A QIGONG INTERPRETATION
- DAO IN ACTION
- DEFENSIVE TACTICS
- DIRTY GROUND
- DR. WU'S HEAD MASSAGE
- ESSENCE OF SHAOLIN WHITE CRANE
- EXPLORING TAI CHI
- FACING VIOLENCE
- FIGHT LIKE A PHYSICIST
- THE FIGHTER'S BODY
- FIGHTER'S FACT BOOK 1&2
- FIGHTING THE PAIN RESISTANT ATTACKER
- FIRST DEFENSE
- FORCE DECISIONS: A CITIZENS GUIDE
- INSIDE TAI CHI
- JUDO ADVANTAGE
- JUJI GATAME ENCYCLOPEDIA
- KARATE SCIENCE
- KEPPAN
- KRAV MAGA COMBATIVES
- KRAV MAGA FUNDAMENTAL STRATEGIES
- KRAV MAGA PROFESSIONAL TACTICS
- KRAV MAGA WEAPON DEFENSES
- LITTLE BLACK BOOK OF VIOLENCE
- LIUHEBAFA FIVE CHARACTER SECRETS
- MARTIAL ARTS OF VIETNAM
- MARTIAL ARTS INSTRUCTION
- MARTIAL WAY AND ITS VIRTUES
- MEDITATIONS ON VIOLENCE
- MERIDIAN QIGONG EXERCISES
- MINDFUL EXERCISE
- MIND INSIDE TAI CHI
- MIND INSIDE YANG STYLE TAI CHI CHUAN
- NORTHERN SHAOLIN SWORD
- OKINAWA'S COMPLETE KARATE SYSTEM: ISSHIN RYU
- PRINCIPLES OF TRADITIONAL CHINESE MEDICINE
- PROTECTOR ETHIC
- QIGONG FOR HEALTH & MARTIAL ARTS
- QIGONG FOR TREATING COMMON AILMENTS
- QIGONG MASSAGE
- QIGONG MEDITATION: EMBRYONIC BREATHING
- QIGONG GRAND CIRCULATION
- QIGONG MEDITATION: SMALL CIRCULATION
- QIGONG, THE SECRET OF YOUTH: DA MO'S CLASSICS
- ROOT OF CHINESE QIGONG
- SAMBO ENCYCLOPEDIA
- SCALING FORCE
- SELF-DEFENSE FOR WOMEN
- SHIN GI TAI: KARATE TRAINING
- SIMPLE CHINESE MEDICINE
- SIMPLE QIGONG EXERCISES FOR HEALTH, 3RD ED.
- SIMPLIFIED TAI CHI CHUAN, 2ND ED.
- SOLO TRAINING 1&2
- SPOTTING DANGER BEFORE IT SPOTS YOU
- SPOTTING DANGER BEFORE IT SPOTS YOUR KIDS
- SPOTTING DANGER BEFORE IT SPOTS YOUR TEENS
- SPOTTING DANGER FOR TRAVELERS
- SUMO FOR MIXED MARTIAL ARTS
- SUNRISE TAI CHI
- SURVIVING ARMED ASSAULTS
- TAE KWON DO: THE KOREAN MARTIAL ART
- TAEKWONDO BLACK BELT POOMSAE
- TAEKWONDO: A PATH TO EXCELLENCE
- TAEKWONDO: ANCIENT WISDOM
- TAEKWONDO: DEFENSE AGAINST WEAPONS
- TAEKWONDO: SPIRIT AND PRACTICE
- TAI CHI BALL QIGONG: FOR HEALTH AND MARTIAL ARTS
- TAI CHI BALL QIGONG
- THE TAI CHI BOOK
- TAI CHI CHIN NA
- TAI CHI CHUAN CLASSICAL YANG STYLE
- TAI CHI CHUAN MARTIAL APPLICATIONS
- TAI CHI CHUAN MARTIAL POWER
- TAI CHI CONCEPTS AND EXPERIMENTS
- TAI CHI DYNAMICS
- TAI CHI FOR DEPRESSION
- TAI CHI IN 10 WEEKS
- TAI CHI PUSH HANDS
- TAI CHI QIGONG
- TAI CHI SECRETS OF THE ANCIENT MASTERS
- TAI CHI SECRETS OF THE WU & LI STYLES
- TAI CHI SECRETS OF THE WU STYLE
- TAI CHI SECRETS OF THE YANG STYLE
- TAI CHI SWORD: CLASSICAL YANG STYLE
- TAI CHI SWORD FOR BEGINNERS
- TAI CHI WALKING
- TAI CHI CHUAN THEORY OF DR. YANG, JWING-MING
- FIGHTING ARTS
- TRADITIONAL CHINESE HEALTH SECRETS
- TRADITIONAL TAEKWONDO
- TRAINING FOR SUDDEN VIOLENCE
- TRIANGLE HOLD ENCYCLOPEDIA
- TRUE WELLNESS SERIES (MIND, HEART, GUT)
- WARRIOR'S MANIFESTO
- WAY OF KATA
- WAY OF SANCHIN KATA
- WAY TO BLACK BELT
- WESTERN HERBS FOR MARTIAL ARTISTS
- WILD GOOSE QIGONG
- WING CHUN IN-DEPTH
- WINNING FIGHTS
- XINGYIQUAN

AND MANY MORE . . .

VIDEOS FROM YMAA

- ANALYSIS OF SHAOLIN CHIN NA
- ART AND SCIENCE OF SELF DEFENSE
- ART AND SCIENCE OF STAFF FIGHTING
- ART AND SCIENCE STICK FIGHTING
- BAGUA FOR BEGINNERS 1 & 2
- BAGUAZHANG: EMEI BAGUAZHANG
- BEGINNER QIGONG FOR WOMEN 1 & 2
- BEGINNER TAI CHI FOR HEALTH
- BREATH MEDICINE
- BIOENERGY TRAINING 1&2
- CHEN TAI CHI CANNON FIST
- CHEN TAI CHI FIRST FORM
- CHEN TAI CHI FOR BEGINNERS
- CHIN NA IN-DEPTH SERIES
- FACING VIOLENCE: 7 THINGS A MARTIAL ARTIST MUST KNOW
- FIVE ANIMAL SPORTS
- FIVE ELEMENTS ENERGY BALANCE
- HEALER WITHIN: MEDICAL QIGONG
- INFIGHTING
- INTRODUCTION TO QI GONG FOR BEGINNERS
- JOINT LOCKS
- KNIFE DEFENSE
- KUNG FU BODY CONDITIONING 1 & 2
- KUNG FU FOR KIDS AND TEENS SERIES
- MERIDIAN QIGONG
- NEIGONG FOR MARTIAL ARTS
- NORTHERN SHAOLIN SWORD
- QI GONG 30-DAY CHALLENGE
- QI GONG FOR ANXIETY
- QI GONG FOR ARMS, WRISTS, AND HANDS
- QIGONG FOR BEGINNERS: FRAGRANCE
- QI GONG FOR BETTER BALANCE
- QI GONG FOR BETTER BREATHING
- QI GONG FOR CANCER
- QI GONG FOR DEPRESSION
- QI GONG FOR ENERGY AND VITALITY
- QI GONG FOR HEADACHES
- QIGONG FOR HEALTH: HEALING QIGONG
- QIGONG FOR HEALTH: IMMUNE SYSTEM
- QI GONG FOR THE HEALTHY HEART
- QI GONG FOR HEALTHY JOINTS
- QI GONG FOR HIGH BLOOD PRESSURE
- QIGONG FOR LONGEVITY
- QI GONG FOR STRONG BONES
- QI GONG FOR THE UPPER BACK AND NECK
- QIGONG FOR WOMEN WITH DAISY LEE
- QIGONG FLOW FOR STRESS & ANXIETY RELIEF
- QIGONG GRAND CIRCULATION
- QIGONG MASSAGE
- QIGONG MINDFULNESS IN MOTION
- QI GONG—THE SEATED WORKOUT
- QIGONG: 15 MINUTES TO HEALTH
- SABER FUNDAMENTAL TRAINING
- SAI TRAINING AND SEQUENCES
- SANCHIN KATA: TRADITIONAL TRAINING FOR KARATE POWER
- SCALING FORCE
- SEARCHING FOR SUPERHUMANS
- SHAOLIN KUNG FU FUNDAMENTAL TRAINING: COURSES 1 & 2
- SHAOLIN LONG FIST KUNG FU BEGINNER—INTERMEDIATE—ADVANCED SERIES
- SHAOLIN SABER: BASIC SEQUENCES
- SHAOLIN STAFF: BASIC SEQUENCES
- SHAOLIN WHITE CRANE GONG FU BASIC TRAINING SERIES
- SHUAI JIAO: KUNG FU WRESTLING
- SIMPLE QIGONG EXERCISES FOR HEALTH
- SIMPLE QIGONG EXERCISES FOR ARTHRITIS RELIEF
- SIMPLE QIGONG EXERCISES FOR BACK PAIN RELIEF
- SIMPLIFIED TAI CHI CHUAN: 24 & 48 POSTURES
- SIMPLIFIED TAI CHI FOR BEGINNERS 48
- SPOTTING DANGER BEFORE IT SPOTS YOU
- SPOTTING DANGER FOR KIDS
- SPOTTING DANGER FOR TEENS
- SUN TAI CHI
- SWORD: FUNDAMENTAL TRAINING
- TAEKWONDO KORYO POOMSAE
- TAI CHI BALL QIGONG SERIES
- TAI CHI BALL WORKOUT FOR BEGINNERS
- TAI CHI CHUAN CLASSICAL YANG STYLE
- TAI CHI FIGHTING SET
- TAI CHI FIT: 24 FORM
- TAI CHI FIT: ALZHEIMER'S PREVENTION
- TAI CHI FIT: CANCER PREVENTION
- TAI CHI FIT FOR VETERANS
- TAI CHI FIT: FOR WOMEN
- TAI CHI FIT: FLOW
- TAI CHI FIT: FUSION BAMBOO
- TAI CHI FIT: FUSION FIRE
- TAI CHI FIT: FUSION IRON
- TAI CHI FIT: HEALTHY BACK SEATED WORKOUT
- TAI CHI FIT: HEALTHY HEART WORKOUT
- TAI CHI FIT IN PARADISE
- TAI CHI FIT: OVER 50
- TAI CHI FIT OVER 50: BALANCE EXERCISES
- TAI CHI FIT OVER 50: SEATED WORKOUT
- TAI CHI FIT OVER 60: GENTLE EXERCISES
- TAI CHI FIT OVER 60: HEALTHY JOINTS
- TAI CHI FIT OVER 60: LIVE LONGER
- TAI CHI FIT: STRENGTH
- TAI CHI FIT: TO GO
- TAI CHI FOR WOMEN
- TAI CHI FUSION: FIRE
- TAI CHI QIGONG
- TAI CHI PRINCIPLES FOR HEALTHY AGING
- TAI CHI PUSHING HANDS SERIES
- TAI CHI SWORD: CLASSICAL YANG STYLE
- TAI CHI SWORD FOR BEGINNERS
- TAI CHI SYMBOL: YIN YANG STICKING HANDS
- TAIJI & SHAOLIN STAFF: FUNDAMENTAL TRAINING
- TAIJI CHIN NA IN-DEPTH
- TAIJI 37 POSTURES MARTIAL APPLICATIONS
- TAIJI SABER CLASSICAL YANG STYLE
- TAIJI WRESTLING
- TRAINING FOR SUDDEN VIOLENCE
- UNDERSTANDING QIGONG SERIES
- WATER STYLE FOR BEGINNERS
- WHITE CRANE HARD & SOFT QIGONG
- YANG TAI CHI FOR BEGINNERS
- YOQI: MICROCOSMIC ORBIT QIGONG
- YOQI QIGONG FOR A HAPPY HEART
- YOQI:QIGONG FLOW FOR HAPPY MIND
- YOQI:QIGONG FLOW FOR INTERNAL ALCHEMY
- YOQI QIGONG FOR HAPPY SPLEEN & STOMACH
- YOQI QIGONG FOR HAPPY KIDNEYS
- YOQI QIGONG FLOW FOR HAPPY LUNGS
- YOQI QIGONG FLOW FOR STRESS RELIEF
- YOQI: QIGONG FLOW TO BOOST IMMUNE SYSTEM

more products available from . . .

YMAA Publication Center, Inc. 楊氏東方文化出版中心

1-800-669-8892 • info@ymaa.com • www.ymaa.com

www.ingramcontent.com/pod-product-compliance
Lightning Source LLC
Chambersburg PA
CBHW081428070526
44586CB00020B/2523